# *The* Soul
## *of* Tomorrow's
## Church

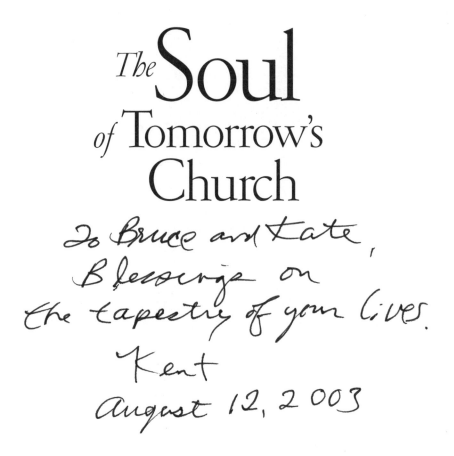

To Bruce and Kate,
Blessings on
the tapestry of your lives.
Kent
August 12, 2003

*More praise for*
## The Soul of Tomorrow's Church

Kent Groff has designed an excellent resource that brings together the whole picture of what it means to practice, with integrity, the presence of God incarnate in a fractured world where liturgy and life have lost their relatedness. Theological seminaries could profit from the interactive structure and content of this extremely well-organized and creatively presented volume.

> **—Melva Wilson Costen**
> Helmar Emil Nielsen Professor of Liturgy and Music
> Interdenominational Theological Center, Atlanta, Georgia
> Author of *African American Christian Worship*

*The Soul of Tomorrow's Church* speaks urgently and insightfully to those concerned for the whole life of the body of Christ. Groff draws together the inner and the outer lives of believers, their past and future, their challenge and their opportunity.

> **—Ray I. Lindquist**
> Pastor, Covington Presbyterian Church, Pavilion, New York

# *The* Soul *of* Tomorrow's Church

WEAVING
Spiritual
Practices
in Ministry
Together

KENT IRA GROFF

UPPER
ROOM BOOKS®
NASHVILLE

THE SOUL OF TOMORROW'S CHURCH
Weaving Spiritual Practices in Ministry Together
Copyright © 2000 by Kent Ira Groff

The Upper Room® Web site http://www.upperroom.org

Cover design: Gore Studio, Inc.
Second printing: 2001

Page 183 constitutes an extension of this copyright page.

Library of Congress Cataloging-in-Publication Data
Groff, Kent Ira.
    The soul of tomorrow's church: weaving spiritual practices in ministry together / Kent Ira
Groff.
              p.  cm.
         Includes bibliographical references.
         ISBN 0-8358-0927-7
         1. Church renewal—Presbyterian Church. 2. Spirituality—Presbyterian Church. I. Title
    BV600.2 .G765 2000                    00-021899
    269—dc21                              CIP


                    Printed in Canada

# Contents

# Leavening the Liturgies

## INDEX OF RESOURCES

## INDEX OF MUSIC

## INDEX OF POEMS

# Acknowledgments

I am grateful for churches I have served—Memorial Presbyterian in Fox Chase, Philadelphia; Twelve Corners Presbyterian, Rochester, New York; and in Pennsylvania: The Presbyterian Church of Waynesboro; Trinity Presbyterian, Berwyn; Paxton Presbyterian, Harrisburg—and Christ Presbyterian, Camp Hill, where I am a parish associate. And I thank the staff, board, and participants of Oasis Ministries for Spiritual Development and all who were part of this project: John Ailstock, Sanford Alwine, Theodore C. Anderson, Nancy Bieber, Geneva M. Butz, Philip Carr-Harris, Rabbi Carl Choper, Elena Delgado, Sr. Marian Delores Frantz, I.H.M., Ray I. Lindquist, Glenn Mitchell, Mary Pinto, Rosalind Y. Powell, Robert P. Richardson, Howard Rice, Kevin Rossiter, Karl Ruttan, Daniel Shultz, Mary Lee Talbot, Emily Wallace, Prudence Yelinek—John M. Seefeldt who assisted with the music and Mary J. Morreale who formatted the music.

I am grateful for a decade of teaching at Lancaster Theological Seminary and of leading seminars at Princeton Theological Seminary. I am grateful to have shared portions of this book there and at Toronto School of Theology, Columbia Theological Seminary, Pittsburgh Theological Seminary, Wesley Theological Seminary, and varied church groups—especially the United Methodist Eastern Pennsylvania Conference and the two-year project of the Jacob Albright District that gave birth to the book.

I appreciate the attentiveness of my editors—JoAnn Miller and Bill Treadway—and the staff family of The Upper Room, founded during the Great Depression to serve as an interdenominational and global catalyst for renewal and still fulfilling that call.

Always I am grateful to my wife, Fredrika, for her perspectives and support. And always guiding me is the ancient wisdom that I am one beggar showing other beggars where to find bread—as others have shown me.

*—Kent Ira Groff*

11

# Gathering Conversation

*CAUTION: DO NOT READ THIS BOOK ALONE! If you are a pastor, find a way to covenant to read and discuss it with lay leaders in your church—as well as with other pastors. If you're a layperson, genuinely invite your pastor to covenant with you and other lay leaders to read and discuss it. (If that seems impossible, seek other friends and another pastor—maybe someone in a specialized ministry.) A church board or community ministry group can study it together. The aim is for lay and clergy disciples to rediscover the common soul of ministry together.*

"If the church doesn't reach out to the community, people won't come. But if people come into our churches and don't sense the presence of God, they're not going to return." This city pastor's comment highlights the crisis and opportunity for twenty-first century disciples. A commissioned lay minister makes the same point: "What drew me to ministry was a sense of God's presence. But now that I serve three rural churches, my spiritual life gets crowded out. When I talk to colleagues about it, they change the subject to stewardship, preaching, whatever. It seems being in ministry is keeping me from God."

The crucial issue here is the heart of the Christian faith itself, the Incarnation: "The Word became flesh" (John 1:14). I want to show how the complex stuff of ministry, which is a barrier to experiencing the simple presence of God, can become a transmitter of God's presence. Within that single focus, the book speaks to several areas of need.

- ❖ *The need to renew the spiritual life of spiritual leaders.* Caught up in *doing* church without *being* church for one another, lay and clergy leaders long for spiritual practices to renew communion and community.
- ❖ *The need for clergy and laity to address conflict together.* Books and seminars designed to "enlighten" pastors often fuel deeper rifts with laity! *The Soul* offers spiritual strategies for church crises.

- ❖ *The need to weave the spiritual with the structural.* Leaders complain that administration stifles the life-giving Spirit, while "spirituality" is often relegated to a corner of church life.

- ❖ *The need to integrate simplicity with complexity.* Church folks feel fragmented by complexity and specialization, finding it hard to connect timeless gospel values and a multiple-choice curriculum, malpractice insurance and the sacredness of Communion.

- ❖ *The need to integrate church growth and spiritual growth.* The church growth agenda can center on "how-to" techniques and quantity rather than depth, while spiritual growth seems disconnected from leadership.

- ❖ *The need to empower part-time and lay ministry.* Here is a creative curriculum resource for lay training programs and smaller churches.

- ❖ *The need for seminarians to integrate theory with practice.* Moving from pew to pulpit, seminary students want to keep the passion of their call alive while engaging in study and ministry. Here is a field education manual.

**Definitions:** *Leadership* and *ministry* refer to a broad base of active disciples—laity and clergy, professional staff and volunteers—who are both seekers after more of God and ministers to a hurting world. When referring to ordained clergy I use the term *pastor.*

**Usages:** The book is written for interactive learning, reflection, prayer, and retreat—especially with clergy and laypersons together, in board meetings or study groups. You may adapt portions for a devotional reading at home or in a committee meeting, a discussion starter or small-group program, a means of sharing between two friends, or a leadership retreat.

**Features:** The *Prelude, Interlude,* and *Postlude* highlight major "threads" woven into the chapters that follow or precede, creating a kind of musical tapestry. *Prayers* and *prayer poems* are interspersed throughout, so that ideas are counterpointed by invitations to experience God's desire for us. *Music* at the beginning of each chapter can be used as personal prayer, as prayer during a business meeting, as responses before or after spoken intercessions—in small groups or public worship. *Leavening the Liturgies* are self-contained, practical methods for enriching five major functions of ministry (worship, administration, education, soul care, and outreach) related to the theme of each chapter—each one listed in the text as (LL #). *Resources* I–IX spell out in more detail a few *Leavening the Liturgies* for personal life and community. A selected bibliography is included, along with a subject index.

*Rationale:* My passion is to make connections between spiritual practices and the nuts and bolts of community life—to draw from the well of Christ contemplatively and actively. "Contemplatively" refers to the title, *The Soul of Tomorrow's Church*, returning to the foundation of the church's mandate: Contemplate divine Love in order to love God, others, and self (Deuteronomy 6:4-5; Mark 12:29-31). "Listen to Love, to love."

"Actively" speaks of the subtitle, *Weaving Spiritual Practices in Ministry Together*. After a year with lay folks in a contemplative program, a theologically articulate pastor said, "I was really skeptical, but I'll tell you this is surely a level playing field." Contemplative practices open us to listen for God in the cries and joys of the world.

# *Prelude*

## Honest-to-God Prayer—and Action

Pray without ceasing, give thanks in all circumstances; for this is
the will of God in Christ Jesus for you.

—**Paul the apostle, 1 Thessalonians 5:17-18**

The day of my spiritual awakening was the day I saw—and knew I
saw—all things in God and God in all things.

—**Mechthild of Magdeburg**

It is necessary to take particular care to begin, if only for a moment,
your exterior actions with this interior gaze and that you do the
same while you are doing them and when you have finished them.

—**Brother Lawrence, *The Practice of the Presence of God***

*Take a few minutes to center yourself and pray.*
> *I would be silent, now,*
> *Lord,*
> *and expectant...*
> *that I may receive the gift I need,*
> *so I may become the gift others need.*

—**Ted Loder, *Guerrillas of Grace***

Every *good* action arises out of contemplation, as a surging waterfall origi-
nates in a still spring. As a weaver contemplates the design for a rug before
and while moving the shuttle, so action and contemplation need not be separate but two movements of a seamless whole. Contemplation is listening
prayer: "Be still, and know that I am God!" (Ps. 46:10). It is *The Practice of
the Presence of God* to be present in the world.[1]

### Prayer as Sabbath *and* Service

Contemplative prayer might be likened to "sabbath" and active prayer to
"service."[2] Prayer as contemplation and prayer as manifestation are like the

roots and the foliage of the tree, one interactive reality—only we keep short-changing the roots and thereby losing the soul of ministry.

As an artist contemplates a landscape and then splashes the colors on the canvas; as a musician contemplates a song and then pens the notes on the score; as a baseball player contemplates the bat's hitting the ball and then swings—so contemplation and manifestation are two movements of one reality.

Like the ballplayer turning toward the ball yet in the same moment turning inward to contemplate and focus, prayer in a paradoxical way is both retreat and involvement—though its rhythm is sometimes longer on one than the other. Yet in an age where bookshelves lean heavily toward self-meditation and self-medication, activists often dismiss prayer as if it is a *turning away* from the real world.

Evelyn Underhill offers a corrective word: "Prayer means turning to Reality."[3] Turning *toward* Reality can mean making silent retreat *or* engaging in social action. In either form prayer is always a turning *around* (*metanoia* in Greek): turning *from* controlling things myself *toward* an inner freedom in God, a movement from willfulness to willingness.[4] In words echoing Thomas Merton, prayer is when we are reconverted. I have been reconverted while building a Habitat for Humanity house, receiving Communion, sitting alone under the stars, reading scripture, conversing with a stranger, participating in a painful exchange at a board meeting.

In the Western world most of us have learned to pray with words, spoken, printed, or inside one's head. Contemplation is akin to the meaning of sabbath, a ceasing from the intensity of words, ideas, and action in order to gain inner perspective. God is the paradigm for prayer: "On the seventh day [God] rested, and was refreshed" (Exod. 31:17). Literally, God "ceased and was re-souled" (*shabat vayanafesh* in Hebrew, AT). The *soul* of ministry is about cultivating times and spaces to be re-souled, about God's life in Christ taking form in us. Here are some ways of cultivating sabbath aptitudes.

❖ Sabbath time is for *prayer*, to practice the presence, to go to God by any means, by any means to let God come to you—away in solitude or present in community.

❖ Sabbath time is for *discernment*, alone or with others—to sharpen the *vision*, to refocus the lens, to cease from doing and ask, Who am I (and who are we) becoming?

❖ Sabbath time is for closing the company store to open the storehouse of *faith stories*, to see ourselves in the divine story that began before time.

- ❖ Sabbath time is for *silence and presence* in the "still point of the turning world"—to fast from the multiplicity of stimuli whose demonic name is Legion if life is unfocused, time to consider the lilies, to notice a falling meteor or a failing neighbor.
- ❖ Sabbath time is for *hospitality*—when strangers interrupting dinner may announce our destiny is like the stars of the heavens and the sand of the seashore (Gen. 18:1-14).

Intentional sabbath practices help us turn to God in all things, in all things to see God, whether in a moment of altruistic service or of narcissistic anger. I invite you to an "ongoing retreat" as you read this book: *Pray always, pray all ways.*

## Honest-to-God Praying
## Two Notes Continually in Discord

Sabbath is an intentional ceasing in time in order to leaven the rest of time with these five aptitudes (see the "tapestry" diagram on page 39). Sabbath is what the poet Rainer Maria Rilke spoke of as "the rest between two notes" that are continually in discord.

What are the two notes in discord for you? What is the rest? Who is the rest? When is the rest? How do you claim the rest? The purpose of intentional sabbath times is to allow the rests to permeate the rhythms of active life—*Living in the Presence*[5] to become fully present in the discords and harmonies of the world. Whatever assists that deep rest, that inner awareness *for you* can rightly be called prayer.

We are distracted because we think we cannot be honest in our praying. Most of us have also vaguely learned to suppress our negative feelings before God. When I felt angry as a youth, I was taught to pray *about* it rather than to pray *the anger itself.* Prayer begins as awareness. Contemplative prayer is being present with God to what is—the beauty of a rosebud, the pain from a car crash, the anger at injustice. Contemplative prayer can notice joy, pain, or anger as valid feelings.

*Notice, offer,* and *listen.* After noticing feelings in relation to an experience, the next step is to offer the "what is" of your life to God. It is not fixing it up first and then turning to God or only offering the "good" part of yourself to God. It is turning to God "just as I am, without one plea," in the words of a hymn, exposing your whole self to be made whole and holy. Prayer is honest-to-God prayer, or it is no prayer. "We cannot hide anything from God without being false to ourselves," observes Howard Rice.[6] Once you have been honest to God and self, you can now listen to your brothers and sisters and listen to God's invitation even through "negative" experiences. *Notice, offer,* and *listen.*

A retreatant once commented to me, "That's what I think sin is—not offering your experience to God, no matter what that experience is." Salvation, then, is continually offering God our life experience, and listening for God's invitation that transforms it into blessing.

### TAME PRAYERS

Most prayers are too tame,
pitying self while others act,
sitting by the pool and feeling lame.

Prayer is an explosion in the heart:
Crazy Noah building an ark,
Abraham bartering with the Lord,
Wild-eyed Isaac on the altar,
Jacob wrestling in the night,
Deborah leading a victory march,
Elijah calling down the rain,
Job taking God to court,
Ruth entreating, "Do not part,"
widows knocking on judges' doors,
outcasts touching Jesus' hem,
a Canaanite mother claiming crumbs,
Mary anointing the Guru's feet:
Jesus crying—Why? My God, my God?—
Startled women at the empty tomb;
Paul in prison singing hymns,
John in exile dreaming dreams.

Prayer is action and retreat—
wherever God and humans meet.

—Kent Ira Groff © 1999

Tame prayers have a lot to do with the vicious conflicts that erupt and rip apart the body of Christ, the family, the workplace. The psalms model honest-to-God praying:

> Contend, O Lord, with those who contend with me;
> fight against those who fight against me! (Psalm 35:1)

If I pray like this in solitude, then I can let God do the fighting—and find myself more able to speak "the truth in love" and "grow up... into Christ" in community (Eph. 4:15).

Genuine sabbath not only personally renews but contains aspects of community *and* solitude, like the front and back sides of a tapestry, like the pattern of Jesus' life. "[Jesus] went out to the mountain to pray; and he spent the night in prayer to God. And when day came, he called his disciples and chose twelve of them, whom he also named apostles" (Luke 6:12-13). Both are sabbath: the intimate night of solitude with God and the intimate community of apostles.

Sabbath practices foster spiritual aptitudes that will leaven structured ministries (Part II). Prayer is not only the prelude, but its contemplative rests are essential for the harmony of this community composition. It is learning to draw from the well of Christ contemplatively *and* actively.

# PART I

_The_ Soul
_of_ Tomorrow's
Church

# CHAPTER ONE

# Restoring the *Soul*
## *Integrity, Passion, Wholeness*

### 1 CORINTHIANS 13

I will show you a still more excellent way. **If I speak in the tongues of mortals and of angels, but do not have love, I am a noisy gong or a clanging cymbal. And if I have prophetic powers, and understand all mysteries and all knowledge, and if I have all faith, so as to remove mountains, but do not have love, I am nothing. If I give away all my possessions, and if I hand over my body so that I may boast, but do not have love, I gain nothing.** Love is patient; love is kind; love is not envious or boastful or arrogant or rude. It does not insist on its own way; it is not irritable or resentful; it does not rejoice in wrongdoing, but rejoices in the truth. It bears all things, believes all things, hopes all things, endures all things. Love never ends. But as for prophecies, they will come to an end; as for tongues, they will cease; as for knowledge, it will come to an end. For we know only in part, and we prophesy only in part; but when the complete comes, the partial will come to an end. When I was a child, I spoke like a child, I thought like a child, I reasoned like a child; when I became an adult, I put an end to childish ways. For now we see in a mirror, dimly, but then we will see face to face. Now I know only in part; then I will know fully, even as I have been fully known. And now faith, hope, and love abide, these three; and the greatest of these is love.

# Turn to God in All Things

Mechthild of Magdeburg, 12th century
Para. Kent Ira Groff, 1991

Kent Ira Groff, 1991

*May be sung by itself, between spoken intercessions,*
*or as a prayer for discernment.*

# Restoring the Soul
## Integrity, Passion, Wholeness

Ministry is contemplation. It is the ongoing unveiling of
reality and the revelation of God's light....The paradox of ministry
indeed is that we will find the God we want to give in the lives of
the people to whom we want to give [God].

—Henri J. M. Nouwen, *Creative Ministry*

The Lord is my shepherd, I shall not want:
who makes me lie down in green pastures,
who leads me beside the still waters,
who restores my soul.

—Psalm 23:1-2, AT

*Come journey together: Invite the Lord to restore the soul of your life
in service—turning to God in the joys, the conflicts, the impasses, and
the new directions.*

As I lead retreats pastors tell me, "I'm here because I can't worship when I
lead worship." I affirm their need for retreat, yet the comment makes me sad.
Can you imagine Aaron the priest or Miriam the prophet saying that? Or
Peter on the day of Pentecost? Or an Eastern Orthodox priest today?

Laypersons who get really involved often fall prey to the same spiritual
dis-ease, with comments such as: "It seems like doing church work is getting
in the way of God." "It's funny, but since I began serving on the board I'm
praying less." "With the feelings I have, I can no longer receive Communion."
How can we still tout "the priesthood of all believers" as so essential? Can we
no longer be priests to one another?

This common attitude belies a gnawing duplicity: How can we who plan and lead worship (lay or clergy) invite others into "the holy of holies" if we are not standing on holy ground ourselves? And if spiritual leaders cannot sense the Presence in *worship,* which exists for the very purpose of experiencing God, then how less likely when we go about the mundane *administration* of church programs! (See chapters 3 and 4.)

The new crisis I see is this: *Ministry itself is getting in the way of re-presenting Christ in the world.* It is a desperate call to restore the *soul* of the church. When I speak of *soul,* I am lifting up three positive qualities related to serious needs of the church:

❖ *Integrity.* When you hear the phrase "selling your soul," it conveys the sense of expediency: "I owe my soul to the company store." We illustrate this crisis in integrity when we lead worship but do not worship or talk love while disparaging others. The soul of ministry together is about practicing what we teach (see Matthew 23:3). It is about spiritual integrity: Can we embody our being in Christ through our doing in the world?

❖ *Passion.* "To put your heart and soul into it" means to do something with passion. Seekers and leaders confess that church is often boring, lacking energy, like salt that has lost its taste. It is lukewarm—neither cold nor hot. In words reminiscent of Kierkegaard, this age will die, not from sin, but from a lack of passion. But passion also means suffering. To discover the passion of Christ in church structures will be painful as old wineskins burst on the way to restoring the integrity and joy of soul.

❖ *Wholeness.* "'Tis all in peeces, all cohaerence gone," wrote John Donne. Ministry in an overspecialized world gets complicated. The *soul* of ministry is about healing personal *and* social fragmentation, finding simplicity in complexity. It is about defragmenting, as when my computer reunifies scattered information. As W. E. B. Du Bois describes in *The Souls of Black Folk,* soul involves a totality of life's suffering and joy. *Soul* is a synonym for *life*: *Nefesh* in Hebrew conveys one's whole being. The Lord is the shepherd who restores my soul. (see Psalm 23:1-2.) "The chief shepherd" is the true Pastor who can also restore the soul of an institution (1 Pet. 5:4).

## The Goal: The Soul of Church

God's call today is for the believing community to re-present these three qualities—the integrity, passion, and wholeness of Christ in the world. It is a call
for this incredible fragile community by its own presence to embody its mission. Over two decades ago former AT&T executive Robert Greenleaf spoke
prophetically in *Servant Leadership*:

> Most charitable institutions, of which the church is one, have tended
> to view the problems of society as "out there," and it was assumed
> that service to the "out there" was the sole justification for their exis-
> tence. Now the view is emerging that one begins "in here," inside the
> serving institution, and makes of *it* a model institution. This model,
> *because it is a thing of beauty, in itself,* becomes a powerful serving force.[7]

Communities of faith yearn for this miracle: to become "a powerful serving
force" even while experiencing turbulent changes in personal and corporate
life. Can the church be the "still point in the turning world"—embodying
change *and* tradition?

## Buzzing Corinthians or Burnt-Out Ephesians

When the Apostle Paul looked at one of the most promising churches he
helped plant, he saw enthusiastic faith, insight, worship, and music, but he
also saw fragmentation, confusion—too much of a good thing. "Has Christ
been divided?" he asked (1 Cor. 1:13). Reflecting on the faith community in
Corinth (1 Cor. 11:17–14:33), he tried to make sense of it, listing church
members' various gifts and strengths. He reflected on the needs and weaknesses: people getting drunk on the Communion wine, sleeping with one
another's loved ones, insisting the spiritual gifts of one were better than
another's and using Greek philosophy to back it up. Right in the middle of
all this confusion he inserted the famous hymn to love, the "more excellent
way" to restore the *soul* of community, to let love permeate every function of
ministry together (1 Corinthians 13):

> If I speak in the tongues of mortals and of angels,
> but do not have love, I am a noisy gong or a clanging cymbal.
> And if I have prophetic powers, and understand
> all mysteries and all knowledge,

and if I have all faith, so as to remove mountains,
but do not have love, I am nothing.

John, exiled on the isle of Patmos, wrote to a different kind of church at Ephesus, one that was discouraged and tired. John affirmed its strengths, its faithfulness, its toil, its patient endurance. Then he added, "But I have this against you, that you have abandoned the love you had at first" (Rev. 2:4).

To the buzzing "evangelical" church with too many bells and whistles, to the bored but faithful "mainline" church, the message is the same: "You have abandoned the soul of ministry. Look at your strengths, confess your weaknesses, and return to your first love."

## Strengths: Five Vital Ministries of Today's Churches

When I look at church communities, whether in Canada or Kenya, India or Indiana, I see five main areas of strength: communities at *worship*, sometimes buzzing, sometimes bored, yet present before God; communities *administering*—organizing to carry out their mission, some with lots of structure, some with almost none, yet motivated by Christ's ministry; communities *educating*, some using fancy learning theories, some using simple story and example, all following glimpses of the master Teacher; communities trying hard to *care for one another*, a few hardly trying, others very trying!—still finding love while being found. Finally, I see communities *reaching out*, somehow locally, somehow globally, yet never completely forgetting: "Feed my sheep....I have other sheep....Go therefore and create disciples among all kinds of people in the world....Just as you did it to even one of the least of these my brothers and sisters, you did it to me" (John 21:17; 10:16; Matt. 28:19, 25:40, adapted).

In varied forms I see contemporary disciples continuing the essential ministries "that Jesus began to do and teach" (Acts 1:1, RSV). Below I offer two biblical examples for each ministry function, based only on the Gospels and the Acts of the Apostles:

1. *Worshiping.* "[Jesus] went to the synagogue on the sabbath day, as was his custom" (Luke 4:16). "Day by day, as [early disciples] spent much time together in the temple, they broke bread at home" (Acts 2:46).

2. *Administering.* Jesus planned his life mission (Luke 4:42-44) and organized others; for example, the mission of the twelve and of the

seventy others (Luke 9 and 10). The early church organized the "diaconate" to administer to people's needs (Acts 6:1-6).

3. *Educating.* "Take my yoke upon you, and *learn* from me" (Matt. 11:29, emphasis added). "They devoted themselves to the apostles' teaching and fellowship, to the breaking of bread and the prayers" (Acts 2:42).

4. *Caring.* "By this everyone will know that you are my disciples, if you have love for one another" (John 13:35). "All who believed were together" and cared for one another "as any had need" (Acts 2:44-45).

5. *Reaching out.* "Go into all the world and proclaim the good news" (Mark 16:15). "And you will be my witnesses in Jerusalem, in all Judea and Samaria, and to the ends of the earth" (Acts 1:8).

Each of these five arenas is grounded in the life of Jesus and of the earliest church.

I view it as a witness to the Resurrection that through five such basic ministry functions (you could name more or fewer), the life-giving Christ becomes present in the world. We become the body of Christ, embodying the new wine that re-presents Jesus' continuing presence right up to the twenty-first century.

The wineskins may be leather, plastic, wooden, glass, or earthenware—taking the form of small rural or city churches, large urban or suburban churches, evangelical or liberal, growing or declining, dying or merging, independent or interdependent, with walls or without walls.

The challenge for today's church is how *not* to focus on new structures but rather on infusing passion into current structures.

We get the order wrong and miss the ardor, creating wineskins before we have new wine. My denomination, the Presbyterian Church (U.S.A), has adopted numerous "secular" systems (having recently approved a fifth national restructure since my ordination in 1967!), yet is still declining in membership and spirit. Since the sixties we have joked about "mainline" churches rearranging the deck chairs on the Titanic.

This "privileged" ship of Christendom, as it has existed since the rule of Constantine the First in the early 300s, is in fact sinking. Christianity became the official religion of the Roman Empire, and disciples of the lonely rabbi Jesus went from being a ridiculed sect thrown to the lions to being privileged allies of royalty. In *The Once and Future Church* Loren B. Mead shows how churches influenced by the West now live in a post-Constantinian era, declining in political and spiritual privileges. Just what form "church" will take in the twenty-first century is not yet clear. But it will need to return to its origins as people of "the Way" (Acts 19:23; 22:4)—*more of a movement than an institution.*

The future church will value function over forms, practices over programs. We have hints from the pre-Constantinian era, from various disestablished branches through the centuries, and from countries where Christians live as minority people. Dietrich Bonhoeffer described it as "religionless Christianity." Howard Thurman encapsulated it in *Jesus and the Disinherited.* Douglas John Hall calls it the "awkward" church.[8] To follow the Titanic metaphor, what is needed is to pay attention, slow down the engines, and get a clear vision of the Christ who goes before us into this uncharted sea.

## Weaknesses: The Loss of Soul and Why

Every crisis is an opportunity for resurrection. Today's crisis is organic, not organizational. We have a lot of wineskins but not much good wine. The salt has lost its taste. It is worse than a failure of nerve. Evangelical churches, like the Corinthian church, have plenty of nerve. The loss of soul is deeper, more like heart than nerve, and has deeper solutions. The first step in discernment is to ask the question: What is going on?

1. *The proliferation of knowledge.* Ministry is so complex that to be a specialist in any one area is to lose the wholeness and holiness of it all. Access to knowledge has taken gigantic leaps in the Internet world. How are we to practice simplicity, what Kierkegaard called singleness of heart, in an age of multiplicity?

2. *Globalization and awareness.* In one week I heard by E-mail from friends in India and in England and wrote to others in Guatemala and Kenya. The NATO nations bombed Kosovo and the world watched refugees' faces, while students bombed Columbine High School in Littleton, Colorado. Who cannot relate national and world violence to domestic youth violence? The Asian economy affects Wall Street. Only a God who makes sense of this global disorientation will be believable. (See chapter 7.)

3. *The end of the OTC ("Only True Church").* The church is not the only place where people go to get their spirituality. (Was it ever?) Yet most denominations once thought they were. Folks take their needs to the self-help bookshelf, the Twelve Step group, or the

Internet, especially younger generations. Hindus and Muslims live next door—making churches feel anxious and defensive.

4. *The explosion of biblical research.* Laypeople are reading scholarly studies about Jesus and are puzzled at what is left of the Jesus they thought they knew. Ministers feel silently de-souled—not knowing how to integrate the stripping down of the Bible with the building up of faith—losing the integrity and passion. (See chapter 5.)

We are in a state of exile as expressed in many of the Psalms: "How shall we sing the Lord's song in a foreign land?" (Ps. 137:4, RSV). Yet people still come to our churches hungering for *ultimacy*, for meaning in their lives, and for *intimacy* with people, with God.

Every year pollsters report in magazines like *U.S. News & World Report, Time, Newsweek,* and *Atlantic Monthly* that large numbers of people in the U.S. have deep religious experiences, but they do not integrate them in religious communities. Our so-called "secular" society is in fact a lot like India, a potpourri of spiritual hotbeds. Current literature about "reaching secular people" fails to address this paradox adequately. In *Fire from Heaven,* Harvey Cox writes about the rise of Pentecostal spirituality; he admits his book *The Secular City,* written in the sixties, missed the mark. "Today, it is secularity, not spirituality, that may be headed for extinction."[9]

A doctoral student at Lancaster Theological Seminary conducted research on "spiritual experiences," in which many staff, students, and faculty (including myself) participated. Even among theologically literate people, only a tiny minority had ever shared these regenerative experiences in a church context or with a pastor. The student's finding resonates with an event from my early ministry. An active church leader came to tell me of experiencing "a sense of Presence" in her dining room. She later confided in my wife that she felt devalued by my discomfort with her disclosure: I had warned her not to let such things get out of hand. Had I known the ancient art of spiritual direction, I could have offered to help her explore and integrate what had happened.

How can we affirm a universal passion for the unique power of the gospel without a crusader attitude? What needs to happen for the church's soul—its *passionate* and *healing* presence—to be restored with *integrity*?

## Restoring the Soul: Claim Identity; Notice Language

As I write the word *restoring*, with its reference to Psalm 23, I notice the similarity to the term *recovering*, popular in today's speech. And having a family member in recovery, I cherish its deep spiritual truth in Twelve Step programs. Can we affirm that these "basement churches" often do more good ministry than the Sunday churches that meet in the upstairs sanctuaries, affirming God's work in both? How can we be salt and light, believing with Jesus that "whoever is not against us is for us" (Mark 9:40)?

Can the church's soul be restored in such a way that claims our unique identity in Christ rather than in demonizing other groups or selling our soul to the culture? Churches unwittingly adopt violent cultural images, such as the word *executive*: to execute is to kill; it also means to carry out orders rather than to discern. Nearly all churches, even pacifists, have followed the culture in adopting this title for their leaders, in preference to the Bible's rich treasury of spiritual images for leadership.

Could such acculturation beginning in the1950s be related to intensity in church conflicts? to weakening spiritual moorings? Why does a book like G. Lloyd Rediger's *Clergy Killers* make such an impact? Lay leaders also come under attack by members and pastors more prepared to "run the church" than to discern the movements of the Spirit. Violent language in titles like *Putting an End to Worship Wars* has the same effect as the parent who calls a child a "brat" while asking the child to act nice. Language shapes our perceptions of that which we name.

I find myself drawing naturally on biblical metaphors: *restoring* fits with *soul*. It illustrates a process I hope will happen as you use this book—that by weaving the threads of the contemplative life into the active life, you will naturally find yourself speaking and thinking differently, like resident aliens, at home *in* the world but not *of* the world, noticing a difference between Christ and culture, while weaving the two appropriately.

This discussion leads us directly back to the challenge for today's church: how *not* to focus on secular models or new structures but instead to focus on ways for the Spirit to infuse existing ministries with new life. Denominations and parachurch organizations like The Alban Institute or Net Results, Inc., and book publishers do well in providing resources for programs of education, stewardship, evangelism, and mission.

Yet among both the bored and the buzzing communities, I see churches that seem to have lost the *soul* of ministry, "holding to the outward form [structures, institutions, and programs] of godliness but denying its [spiritual] power" (2 Tim. 3:5). What would it look like for the outward forms to be enfleshed with the power of love?

# CHAPTER TWO

# Contemplative Practices for Church Programs

## 1 CORINTHIANS 13

**I will show you a still more excellent way.** If I speak in the tongues of mortals and of angels, but do not have love, I am a noisy gong or a clanging cymbal. And if I have prophetic powers, and understand all mysteries and all knowledge, and if I have all faith, so as to remove mountains, but do not have love, I am nothing. If I give away all my possessions, and if I hand over my body so that I may boast, but do not have love, I gain nothing. **Love is patient; love is kind; love is not envious or boastful or arrogant or rude. It does not insist on its own way; it is not irritable or resentful; it does not rejoice in wrongdoing, but rejoices in the truth. It bears all things, believes all things, hopes all things, endures all things. Love never ends.** But as for prophecies, they will come to an end; as for tongues, they will cease; as for knowledge, it will come to an end. For we know only in part, and we prophesy only in part; but when the complete comes, the partial will come to an end. When I was a child, I spoke like a child, I thought like a child, I reasoned like a child; when I became an adult, I put an end to childish ways. **For now we see in a mirror, dimly, but then we will see face to face. Now I know only in part; then I will know fully, even as I have been fully known. And now faith, hope, and love abide, these three; and the greatest of these is love.**

# My Soul Is Like a Weaned Child

Kent Ira Groff, 1996
From Psalm 131:2

Kent Ira Groff, 2000

*May be sung by itself; between spoken intercessions; or before, between, and after verses of Psalm 131.*

Text and music © Kent Ira Groff, 2000.

# Contemplative Practices
## For Church Programs

Above all, clothe yourselves with love, which binds everything
together in perfect harmony.

—Colossians 3:14

The life of each one of us is, as it were, woven of those two
threads: the thread of inward development, through which our
ideas and affections and our human and religious attitudes are
gradually formed; and the thread of outward success by which we
always find ourselves at the exact point where the whole sum of
the forces of the universe meet together to work in us the effect
which God desires.

—Teilhard de Chardin, *The Divine Milieu*

*O God, that at all times you may find me as you desire me and where
you would have me be, that you may lay hold on me fully, both by the
Within and the Without of myself, grant that I may never break this
double thread of my life.*

—Teilhard de Chardin

Love binds everything together in harmony, and the garment being woven
has qualities of compassion and equality, within and without. I propose we
focus our energies on weaving ancient practices with contemporary ministries.
We have already been weaving if you look carefully. Caring for one another
is a key to outreach: "By this everyone will know that you are my disciples,
if you have love for one another" (John 13:35). "The apostles' teaching" is not
an isolated program of education, but in Acts 2:42 is bound together by devotion and crafted into a four-strand masterpiece:

The apostle's teaching *and* fellowship,
the breaking of bread *and* the prayers.

## Weaving the Spiritual with the Structural

If the twentieth century's major church mistake was to focus on structures while ignoring spirituality, then much of what is happening now seems to be focusing on spirituality while ignoring structures. To split the two misses the miracle of Incarnation. While structures that ignore spirituality are lifeless, spirituality that disregards structures is disembodied.

John Wesley spoke of spiritual practices as "methods," from which his followers were dubbed "Methodists." Methods have no value in themselves, except, like conduits in a desert, to carry the life-giving gospel of love to places of need.

My intent is not to create another program but to highlight the love that emerges in the weaving. The great distortion of mystical experience is to make idols out of *techniques*—a word I refuse to use. *Techniques* sound so mechanical: Use this lever and out pops God for this occasion; use that one for another. We can be addicted to dead forms or dead functions and miss the new life.

To focus on fancy threads is to miss the process of weaving the garment with love. You can trade one set of bells and whistles for another and still end up with a noisy gong or a clanging cymbal without the harmony of love. Can we weave life-giving spiritual practices into structured programs of the church in such a genuine fashion that we do not end up with another "how-to" manual?

"Let love be genuine," writes Paul (Rom. 12:9). Genuine mysticism is falling in love with God and with the world God loves. One theme runs throughout the message of scripture: "Listen to Love, to love." It is the most important Hebrew prayer, named for the first word, the *Shema*: "Listen, O people of God: The Lord our God, the Lord is one. You shall love..." (Deut. 6:4, AT). Listen to how deeply God loves you—and then love God and your neighbor as yourself. In the words of an ancient spiritual guide, "To influence you must love, to love you must pray." This is the gospel of Jesus. It is the contemplative active life.

Such "practice-oriented" faith communities will wed tradition with experience. Robert Wuthnow writes, "[They] will strive to give members both roots and wings—roots to ground them solidly in the traditions of their particular faith, wings to explore their own talents and the mysteries of the sacred."[10]

## Weaving: Five Spiritual Aptitudes

The goal is to allow the form of Jesus the Christ to take shape in the believer and the believing community. It is to experience the soul of Christ's integrity, passion, and wholeness in five basic functions of community: *worship, administration, education, soul care,* and *outreach.* In varied forms these are the foundational mandates of ministry, so let us view these as the warp, the vertical threads in the tapestry.

Interfaced with these are five horizontal threads, the weft of essential spiritual aptitudes that open us for God to restore the soul of ministry: *prayer, discernment-vision, faith stories, silence-presence,* and *hospitality.* There can be fewer or more, yet these five practices reflect the pattern of Christ's life as contemplative threads are woven into the warp of active ministry. The pattern created is a twill, known for its durability, flexibility, and potential variety of horizontal threads. (See the bookmark flap.) The task of each new generation is to weave its life into the eternal worshiping, organizing, teaching, caring, witnessing communion of saints.

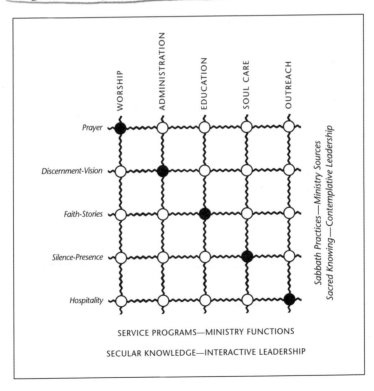

1. *Prayer* is the contemplative thread woven into every aspect of the life of the believer and the believing community: Turn to God in all things, in all things to see God.[11] While prayer is especially part of worshiping, it is also part of educating ("Lord, teach us to pray" Luke 11:1), administering, caring, and reaching out.

2. *Discernment* becomes the basic means for personal and corporate *vision*. Contemplative decision making means listening attentively with one ear to the voice of God through scripture, tradition, reason, and experience—and with the other ear to the cries and hopes of the world. Discernment is the essence of administration, but it is woven throughout all the other ministry areas too, as, for example, in discerning appropriate worship and music styles for a congregation.

3. *Faith stories* are the fruit of finding traces of God's presence in joy and pain—or the longing for God's presence. Faith finding and faith sharing become an "educational habit" in all contexts of church, work, family, and personal life too through the use of a journal. Incorporating faith stories in community will require the sacrifice of give and take by leaders and members, especially in the heart of public worship and so many administrative meetings.

4. *Silence and presence* are the contemplative bedrock for listening to divine Love in order to love. The ballast of stillness balances the latest technological novelties, church-growth techniques, and information explosion—all of which threaten to veer the church off its charted course. Silence enriches personal life but also has a corporate dimension in the church's ministries: It is the key in discernment for planning and decision making. Silence is the prerequisite for meaningful presence, and simply being present to God and another brother or sister grounds any authentic soul care.

5. *Hospitality* is "giving-receiving" in a simultaneous, creative interaction; it also means we are never in mission alone. It is the essential habit of mutuality at the core of the life-giving community: "No church entered into partnership with me in giving and receiving except you only" (Phil. 4:15, RSV). "Giving without receiving is always a downward gesture," goes an anonymous proverb. It is a danger of mission work to act out of a subtly superior position. A Franciscan attitude of simplicity needs to permeate every sphere of community: "In giving…we receive."

## Community and Solitude
## Front and Back of the Tapestry

I invite you now to allow the Spirit to begin to weave these five threads of prayer, discernment, faith stories, silence, and hospitality into every context of your life and your community until you experience their tones while worshiping, organizing, educating, caring for one another, and reaching out to the world.

The aim is to make space for contemplative practices in the active life of community, while at the same time cultivating them in solitude. As the Christ-life takes form in us, so this tapestry's public dimensions (the front side) and private dimensions (the back side) are interfaced. The trumpeter who does not practice has trouble playing in the band, yet the band also helps the trumpeter to practice. (See page 39.)

## Standing Back from the Loom

The weaving metaphor restores the loom of ministry to the bedrock of grace, protecting against the intense control evident in some of the church growth movement. "Discover the leverage points, focus on them, and align everything around them," declares William Easum, who otherwise offers helpful ideas for dealing with conflictual members.[12] But what attitudes come to mind when you hear "leverage points?" And how does it feel to be a member of a *driven* church—whether a seeker-driven, mission-driven, or purpose-driven church? "For freedom Christ has set us free" from controlling or being controlled (Gal. 5:1).

Weaving conveys a work in process that returns spiritual formation to its foundation of grace: simply placing ourselves in a context where the divine Weaver can create and recreate the work of art. Then church growth and spiritual growth can engage each other.

Every tapestry needs a background, a context so it can be appreciated and responded to as a work of art. Our background is a global context—one that calls us to listen simultaneously to the cry of God's love and the cry of the world. And to ignore this global background in our programs is to betray the humanity of Jesus and one's own soul.

A colleague told me of an old German proverb, which I have adapted from a couple of versions: "Begin to weave, and God will show you the pattern—and give you the thread." As I write, ideas emerge out of scarcity and weave themselves in abundance. With that image of abundance out of scarcity, here is my prayer for you as you read. You may use it for personal prayer or in a family or community context, pausing (after the phrase "in solidarity with all") to invite people to name their concerns for specific persons, institutions, and places. Prayers like this can help introduce others to a combination of verbal prayer and contemplative prayer.

BEGIN TO
WEAVE, AND
GOD WILL SHOW
YOU THE PATTERN
AND GIVE YOU
THE THREAD.
*Adapted from
a German proverb.*
May I begin, O God—merely begin, and begin
again to weave the essential habits of the heart
in this my life... in this our community....
May I begin by listening... listening
to the rapid shuttle in my heart...
to the slow shuttle of my breathing...
to the clatter and pain of the world...
to your still small voice—Peace:
Be still... and know that I am God...
Be still... and know that I am God...
Be still... and know that I am God...
Let me be open to surprise as you show
the unique pattern for my life to grow
in solitude... and in solidarity with all....
[Name persons... institutions... places....]
Weave your Love throughout my life,
till I wear it like a well-worn garment,
suited well for my unique frame within,
suited to changes of time and place without,
keeping me secure in your changeless Love
and always facing toward the world with hope;
in the name of Jesus and for the sake of the world.
AMEN—MAY IT BE SO.

—**Kent Ira Groff** © 1999

(Permission is granted to photocopy this prayer for one-time use.)

# *Interlude*

## Soul and "Multiple Intelligences"

What are some ways for the *soul* to be restored for varied learning styles and personality types, cultural and economic backgrounds, masculine and feminine perspectives? Howard Gardner's theory of multiple intelligences offers a holistic frame for this tapestry. Some forms of intelligence are highly developed in a person, others less; everyone has some aptitude in each.[13]

1. LINGUISTIC INTELLIGENCE, oral or written, sign or Braille, is essential for human survival. The community of faith is where we learn the language of love through scriptures, spiritual readings, sermons, prayers, liturgies.

2. LOGICAL/MATHEMATICAL INTELLIGENCE is highly valued in the Western church. Witness thinkers like Aquinas and Calvin, C. S. Lewis and Evelyn Underhill. We need such models for theo*logical* insight: "faith seeking understanding," as Anselm of Canterbury put it.

3. SPATIAL INTELLIGENCE refers not only to conceptualizing space as an architect might do but also to inner space, exploring imagination as well as the outer space of geography and galaxies—and designing room space for optimal learning.

4. MUSICAL INTELLIGENCE, from psalms to Gregorian to Taizé chants to Reformation hymns to African American spirituals to gospel praise choruses, does not depend on formal music education. As Augustine said, "One who sings prays twice."

5. KINESTHETIC INTELLIGENCE connects individual and community: with the flick of the maestro's hands, the symphony begins; in the flailing of the umpire's arms, a ball game is turned upside down. The language of gestures is embodied meaning. It is an invitation to play and to pray: folding or lifting hands, kneeling, bowing.

6. INTERPERSONAL INTELLIGENCE is a well-developed mode of spiritual growth for extroverts: being with God in community. By

the same token, introverts who struggle in large-group conversations are blessed by focusing attention on just one other— the ancient art of spiritual friendship, or more formally, spiritual direction.

7. INTRAPERSONAL INTELLIGENCE is the introvert's preferred mode of spiritual growth: being with God in solitude. Silence is the most neglected form of intelligence in technological societies. Learning and praying in solitude is a corrective for the extrovert, and it preserves the sanity of the introvert.

8. NATURALIST INTELLIGENCE (recently added by Gardner) is at home in Christian spirituality: "The whole creation has been groaning in labor pains" (Rom. 8:22). God reveals Godself through the book of scripture and the book of nature: patterns of dying and rising, devastation and renewal, violence and beauty.

These eight *Frames of Mind* provide a practical tool for assessing "soul" in each spiritual practice, such as hospitality: Is it heavy on interpersonal talk and ideas? Is there spaciousness for intrapersonal solitude? for movement? for exploring geography, nature, music? Likewise these frames can be used to assess any of the five ministry functions, such as worship (see LL 36 and 37).

There are no separate categories for "spiritual" or "emotional" intelligence, because the Word can be enfleshed with passion in every sphere of life. This framework is both liberating and healing. The tendency of Western communication toward linguistic and logical modes cramps the souls of many genuine God-seekers. "The same shoe doesn't fit every foot," and this model opens up varied options to find and follow the Lord of life while being found. It invites us to learn to yearn always—and all ways. In the following chapters we will draw on these options to show many ways the soul can be restored to church life.

# PART II

*Weaving*
Spiritual
Practices
*in Ministry*
Together

# CHAPTER THREE

# The Soul of Worship
## The Liturgies of Our Lives

ROMANS 12

**I appeal to you therefore, brothers and sisters, by the mercies of God, to present your bodies as a living sacrifice, holy and acceptable to God, which is your spiritual worship.** Do not be conformed to this world, but be transformed by the renewing of your minds, so that you may discern what is the will of God—what is good and acceptable and perfect. For by the grace given to me I say to everyone among you not to think of yourself more highly than you ought to think, but to think with sober judgment, each according to the measure of faith that God has assigned. **For as in one body we have many members, and not all the members have the same function, so we, who are many, are one body in Christ, and individually we are members one of another. We have gifts that differ according to the grace given to us: prophecy, in proportion to faith; ministry, in ministering; the teacher, in teaching; the exhorter, in exhortation; the giver, in generosity; the leader, in diligence; the compassionate, in cheerfulness. Let love be genuine;** hate what is evil, hold fast to what is good; love one another with mutual affection; outdo one another in showing honor. Do not lag in zeal, be ardent in spirit, serve the Lord. Rejoice in hope, be patient in suffering, persevere in prayer. Contribute to the needs of the saints; extend hospitality to strangers. Bless those who persecute you; bless and do not curse them. **Rejoice with those who rejoice, weep with those who weep.** Live in harmony with one another; do not be haughty, but associate with the lowly; do not claim to be wiser than you are. Do not repay anyone evil for evil, but take thought for what is noble in the sight of all. If it is possible, so far as it depends on you, live peaceably with all. Beloved, never avenge yourselves, but leave room for the wrath of God; for it is written, "Vengeance is mine, I will repay, says the Lord." No, "if your enemies are hungry, feed them; if they are thirsty, give them something to drink; for by doing this you will heap burning coals on their heads." Do not be overcome by evil, but overcome evil with good.

# Here Am I

Kent Ira Groff, 1996
From Luke 1:38

Kent Ira Groff, 2000

Here am I, the ser- vant of the Lord: Let it

be with me ac- cor-ding to your Word. —

*May be sung by itself, between spoken intercessions,
or as a response to the reading of scripture.*

# The Soul of Worship
## The Liturgies of Our Lives

*Leitourgía—*
"Celebrating God's work in people's lives"

We keep a troubled vigil at the bedside of the world....Thus we
clutch the moment of intimacy in worship when we become
momentarily a part of a larger whole, a fleeting strength, which we
pit against all the darkness and the dread of our times.

—Howard Thurman, *The Inward Journey*

In each week's worship service, we seek to have one element that
expands the texture and richness of worship beyond the usual
music and message. This third component of worship involves
storytelling, both fictional (through drama) and real-life (through
verbal testimonies and interviews). Storytelling shows how the
gospel makes a difference in people's day-to-day lives.

—Paul Nixon, *Net Results* 20 (no. 2)

*Take a few minutes to pray. Breathe slowly. Center yourself. Ask to
be present to God as you read and for new ways to practice the Presence in your own liturgies of worship and work.*

How can worship be transformed into a masterpiece of service to one another
*and* the world? And how can our mundane work in the world be transformed
into worship?

That is the purpose of "the soul of worship" and of this book—to leaven
the liturgies of our lives, alone and together, with awareness of the sacred.
This transformation is the Incarnation: God in Christ enfleshed in every arena

49

of life. It is the paschal mystery: Worship happens when we offer the pain of our lives and of the world to be transformed into hope. Nothing dramatizes this transformation more vividly than the Eucharist, where the signs of brokenness become the signs of blessing. Thus no experience, however profane or mundane, lies outside the arc of Christ's redemption.

Note: Each of the following five chapters begins with the contemplative practice crucial to that ministry function, then weaves the other four in sequence. For example, worship starts with prayer, followed by discernment-vision, faith stories, silence-presence, and hospitality. In administration we start with discernment-vision, then weave each of the others in sequence. (Use the bookmark flap as a guide for your reading.)

### Restoring the Soul of Worship

To restore the soul of worship is to allow the integrity, passion, and healing presence of Christ to shape us, trusting fleeting glimpses of wholeness for our fragmented selves and world. Worship becomes a "habit of being," to use a phrase from Flannery O'Connor, "something in which the whole personality takes part—the conscious as well as the unconscious mind."[14] To re-soul worship is to wed the verbal language of the Word proclaimed (left brain) with the body language of the Word dramatized (right brain) in sacraments, music, movement, and gestures. It is to incorporate these five essential "habits of the heart" beginning in the very heart and soul of Christian community.

## 1. Praying—*and* Leading Worship

Worship is the vital nerve that nurtures the muscles of our faith. Weaving contemplative practices in the fabric of worship rejuvenates the ligaments and liturgies of our lives. Like the front and backsides of the tapestry, the goal of liturgy is to let the pattern of Jesus' life shape us. As prayer in community enlivens solitude, prayer in solitude enlivens community.

The New Testament uses several words to signify worship. *Latreuein* means "to serve," emphasizing the soul's surrender to God. *Proskunein* literally means "to kiss toward" or "to bow down," often prostrate, and is still practiced in Mid-Eastern and Asian cultures. Both words point to worship as holistic and multisensual—involving multiple intelligences. Genuine prayer pays attention to our longings, and life-giving rituals help us notice God in our surroundings. While ritual*ism* can stifle the spirit, creative ritual embodies our longings, like greeting a friend after a long separation. Healthy ritual allows a secular person to participate in the holy "as dancing allows the tongue-tied man a ceremony of love," as Andre Dubus expressed it in "A Father's Story."[15] A key term for worship in the New Testament is "liturgy," *leitourgía,* literally "the people's work" (*laos + erga*). Our English word *laity* is the cousin of the Greek *laos,* so liturgy by definition is a lay-centered activity! But there is something even deeper here. Worship is not celebrating *our* works: "For it is God who is at work in you, enabling you both to will and to work for [God's] good pleasure" (Phil. 2:13). *Genuine worship is celebrating God's work in people's lives!*

Liturgy can refer to the priest's holy service of worship in the temple (Zechariah in Luke 1:23). But it is also a double thread wrapped in human service to others, simultaneously offered as thanksgiving (Eucharist) to God. Paul compliments the enthusiastic Corinthians for their financial generosity: "For this service (*diakonía*) of worship (*leitourgía*) not only supplies the needs of the saints but also overflows with many thanksgivings (*eucharistia*—Eucharist!) to God" (2 Cor. 9:12, AT). This text embodies Catholic *and* Quaker theology: a gift shared out of gratitude with people in need is sacramental! It is the paradigm of liturgy as the *service* of *worship.*

## Worshiping While Laypeople Lead Worship

Since the 1960s abundant resources have been produced "to equip the saints for the work of the ministry" (Eph. 4:12). Yet when this equipping happens in significant ways, theologically trained pastors often become ill at ease.

In a church where the congregation was invited to share joys and concerns, one morning the lay folks began actually to pray aloud. They offered such sacred prayers that the atmosphere was charged with a holy silence. But as the prayers concluded, the pastor was caught off guard and immediately began announcing the upcoming garage sale.

What a golden crisis-opportunity to train laypeople to offer "the prayers of the people"! That is exactly what the pastor, Dr. Geneva M. Butz, and the people have done at Old First Reformed Church (United Church of Christ) in downtown Philadelphia. (See LL 44, "Participatory Prayers.")

## Worshiping While Leading Worship: Two Parables

How can the worship leader worship? This question is crucial for restoring the soul of worship, not just for clergy. Many churches now have lay teams leading contemporary services, where monitoring sound and lighting can readily distract the focus from the worship of God to putting on a good show. Can a lay reader be prayerful (or playful!) as latecomers enter?

I have worshiped in Eastern Orthodox, Catholic, Indian, African and African American, Pentecostal, and Hispanic services where the issue of leaders worshiping would never be raised—so involved in the worship were the clergy, musicians, and lay leaders themselves. Since this quality of Presence is a habit of art, more caught than taught, I offer two "secular" parables in which the artist and the art become one.

- ❖ A cook in Iowa simultaneously relishes the aromas and follows a complicated gourmet recipe that has its origins among his ancient Ethiopian peasant ancestors. While savoring and sampling food, he meticulously measures the main ingredients, guesses at the herbs, regulates the heat, and feels connected to his grandmother's spirit as he uses her method for boiling down the vegetables so the natural sugar remains intact. When the guests suddenly appear at the door and comment on the pungent aroma, he confesses he has lost track of the time and forgotten his body reeks of garlic.

- ❖ An astronomer in California gets to see one of nature's biggest shows of the century while fine-tuning the high-tech controls on the Hubble space telescope. Simultaneously getting directions from her assistant, calibrating a new lens, and setting the computer controls for infinity, her spine tingles as she views the latest in a series of Gamma Ray Bursts—this particular GRB originating nine billion light-years away! Returning to her apartment, she recalls connections with research from ancient observatories in India and Egypt, and plans her lecture describing the amazing GRB to her graduate students the next day. She falls asleep exhausted, yet knowing she has at once stepped forward and backward in time.

## Beyond Parables: Designing Your Own Worship Lab

I trust these parables to create inner connections with ancient liturgies that date back from early Israel through the book of Revelation, down to the present in your own denominational and personal liturgies. They illustrate the Eucharist: When the art and artist become one, energy fuses with exhaustion; stillness is found in noise, joy in sacrifice. Below I suggest a specific exercise to cultivate a hearing heart, to train our souls to be attentive to God amid distractions in work and worship.

❧ **The Sounds of Silence.** (LL 1) Practice sitting in silence: close your eyes and slow down your breathing. Meditate on a short phrase of scripture such as "Be still, and know…" (Ps. 46:10) or repeat a short prayer word like *Maranatha* ("our Lord come"), *amor* ("love"), *Abba*, or *manna*. If thoughts of people and problems come to mind, bless them gently and let them go as intercessory prayers. Enjoy silence with no words. Practice this for several minutes each week, imagining yourself and others being loved by God.

❖ **Adaptation:** Now find a really noisy place, or turn up a rock radio station. Try returning to the silence: slow down your breathing, listen beneath and beyond the noises. See if you can imagine yourself being loved by God amid the noise or invite the distractions into your prayers. Conclude by opening your eyes and reflecting on this experience.

During a sabbatical, I was on a thirty-day retreat in a Jesuit center in Jamshedpur, India. But instead of the quiet I longed for, it was full of noise—people, animals, technology, loud music. It seemed like an impossible challenge to learn to meditate beneath distractions. Then one day while trying to picture Jesus' triumphal entry into Jerusalem, I began to hear the braying of animals, shouts of children, and whirring of sirens as noises in Jesus' joyous parade into the city. Here is a summary from my journal:

### HOUNDING SOUNDS

Hollywood cannot create this set:
you only close your eyes and let
such dogged sounds be holy hounds
of heaven in a temple of contemplation.

—**Kent Ira Groff** © 1999

Try practicing the above method in worship itself: Slow the pace, trust in grace, allow silent spaces to pause and pray as a worship leader or worshiper.

Finally, surrender the burden of perfectionism: remember and remind others that all our worship is only a *rehearsal* for joining the chorus of the morning stars and the angels and saints. (Mention this in "Cueing Worship," LL 3 below.)

A vital thread in worship is discernment *before* (planning), *after* (evaluating), and *during* the service itself: What is the appropriate response in this moment? African American and Hispanic cultures offer rich traditions of discerning needs and gifts in the service of God's people right in worship.

## 2. Discerning Ways of Worshiping

*Genuine worship is celebrating God's work in people's lives*! What would it mean to use this thought as a lens for discerning meaningful worship? A host of issues calls for practicing this habit of discernment for *your* community. Who attends? Who do you want to attend? How do their needs affect the form and content, the place and space, times and accessibility? How do you discern the frequency of Communion in the context of your community and in the context of biblical and church traditions?[16]

This book cannot give a full-fledged theology and practice for worship—or for any of the five functions of church life. Rather it is a catalyst to help mine your own resources. Below I explore three pressing issues for worship: moving from entertainment to involvement, through tradition to contemporary and contemplative, and with varied music styles.

### *From Entertainment to Involvement*

The first arena of discernment as it relates to worship is not whether you have liturgical worship, but how your liturgy can become more participatory—whether Mennonite or Methodist. The goal of worship is a movement from entertainment to involvement. What practices can help people to weave the liturgies of their lives to become at once a service to one another and God? Good performance, whether sermon or anthem, drama or dance, can also be participatory if it articulates the devotion or the questions of other worshipers.[17] Eugene Peterson writes the following:

> I want to use the term "liturgy" to refer to the intent and practice of Christians to pull everything in and out of the sanctuary into the life of worship, situate everything past and present coherently as an act of worship.[18]

To pull everything in and out of the sanctuary into the life of worship on this liturgical loom is to create worship that is participatory, cross-cultural, and intergenerational. Here are some methods to move from entertainment to involvement.

- **Music across Cultures (LL 2)** Through cross-cultural music we can practice hospitality and participate in Jesus' resurrection, transcending racial and geographical boundaries in a living communion of saints. Use a description such as this to "cue" worship next time you use a song from another culture.

- **Cueing Worship (LL 3)** Try weaving brief transitions into your own church's liturgies, cues to give meaning, often humorously, often spontaneously: interpret a gesture or a phrase from your liturgy; highlight a line of the Lord's Prayer related to the sermon theme. Pause during a hymn (alert the accompanist) to suggest: "Sing this verse as an intercessory prayer for a person or cause that concerns you"—or for a concern that is on everyone's mind.

- **Choirs as the "Chief Liturgists" (LL 4)** Restore the choirs of children, youth, adults to their rightful place, inviting them to be the leading prompters for all aspects of the people's worship. Enlist choir leadership to break the ice when introducing participatory options in worship: speaking or whispering joys and concerns aloud, creating alternative applause, passing the peace, singing a spiritual spontaneously in the middle of a sermon. (If you are a music director, work for ways to incorporate faith sharing and prayer in rehearsals, such as singing an anthem as an intercession for the monthly church board meeting that week or singing a chant followed by a time to offer concerns.)

- **To Applaud—or Not to Applaud? (LL 5)** Discernment involves listening beneath the surface to a deeper desire: *People want to respond verbally or kinesthetically to joy in worship.* Prompt people with creative yet traditional options: Encourage the spoken "Amen!" or "Yes!" (with a movement of one hand and arm downward). Invite a silent "wave" offering, sign language for applause. Or try lifting folded hands upward with a couple of quick claps, *directing applause to God on behalf of people's gifts!*

### Through Tradition to Contemplative and Contemporary

The second arena is discerning creative solutions to the volatile worship debates that are causing trouble at the table with music as the centerpiece. I see three options.

The first is to hold on to frozen traditional*ism* until a church dies or merges. The second is to revitalize meaningful traditional worship and also add a contemporary service—attracting seekers, increasing attendance and participation. This risks polarization of the community and losing the ballast of healthy tradition in the contemporary service. A third way is to design "complementary worship," utilizing your own liturgical skeleton while enriching connective tissues with new forms—and "new" but neglected traditions, such as renewal of baptism, anointing with oil, kneeling to pray, or processing with the Bible or a cross.

What would such "both/and" worship look like—liturgy that is both traditional and fresh, liturgical and free church, evangelically centered and socially concerned, with praise choruses and stately hymns?—what Robert Webber calls "ancient-future worship." Option two can be a bridge until, in time, liturgies evolve with greater integration and integrity.

I call this third way "complementary worship." It is both contemplative and contemporary, calling us to discern a deeper vision than the bland sound of "blended worship."

"Sit, stand, or kneel." These words are printed in the bulletins of some Episcopal churches giving freedom to the worshipers who come from different traditions. (Blended worship would settle for "sit.") Here is a tiny parable of what needs to happen in the post-Constantinian era. It echoes the Moravian tradition: unity in essentials, liberty in nonessentials, and charity in all things.

> ↝ **Authentic Worship for Sound-Byte Culture (LL 6)** Traditional oral cultures that communicate with brief proverbs and today's sound-byte culture have much in common as increasingly many youth and adults experience short attention spans. Whether or not officially diagnosed with ADD (Attention Deficit Disorder), many with "theological ADD" tune out of long periods in worship. Try designing your personal worship with brief but unified segments—as a lab to design corporate complementary worship. For example:
>
> ❖ Invite persons to repeat a short verse of scripture together during a sermon or before a prayer;
>
> ❖ Break creeds or faith statements said in unison into a series of questions and answers;
>
> ❖ Repeat a chant or praise chorus between spoken prayers of thanksgiving or intercession (see LL 44, "Participatory Prayers").
>
> Linking a variety of meaningful prayer forms with integrity (using multiple intelligences as a guide) can unite generations. Try it out in small groups of varying ages.

## *With Varied Music Styles: Restoring Joy in Sacrifice*

The term *Generation X* feels dismissive to many youth, so I speak of Generation Y, since youth will always have differing styles from elders. Music both divides and bridges the generations. To hold our own choices lightly with willingness to sacrifice for the common good is the spiritual ground of discernment. *"Present your bodies as a living sacrifice...*which is your spiritual worship... *so that you may discern* what is the will of God—what is good and acceptable and perfect" (Romans 12:1-2, emphasis added).

Gandhi listed "worship without sacrifice" as one of seven social sins. Experiencing drums may be a sacrifice for the senior generation, while singing a yesteryear's hymn may be a sacrifice for Generation Y, something you might note in "Cueing Worship" (LL 3). You can hear a clear sign of the times from a car near you sitting at nearly any red light: "Bum ba da...bum ba da... bum ba da...bum...." Musicologist Brian Wren has pointed out that in *popular* music, whatever its style—folk, Broadway, mountain, country, rock, jazz— "the one thing they all have in common is the importance of rhythm." Whereas traditional Euro-American hymns have given primacy to harmony, popular and native music in all cultures have given primacy to rhythm. I translate this into one clear rubric:

> *We need to include percussion and some instrument(s) other than a pipe organ for a portion of every service of worship to reflect the integrity, passion, and wholeness of Christ in the twenty-first century.*

"Rhythm tries to move you bodily; it is not just a head trip," as Wren notes.[19] No wonder that from forever and everywhere the drum has been an instrument of healing, reminiscent of the heartbeat of God—used in primal caves, rock bands, and sophisticated symphonies. The pipe organ is a wonderful instrument, which I love to play myself. But in combining many instruments in one, it decreased participation of the many. Happily, the trend is reversing. The organ is being used alongside or with the accompaniment of keyboard, flute, strings, guitar, horn, percussion and with a variety of music styles: pop, jazz, classical, rock, country, chants, praise choruses, gospel.

In attending churches in the Middle East, Africa, India and the Virgin Islands, I have come away with a sad feeling when worship is constricted by musical vestiges from Euro-American culture. In contrast, since Vatican II, Catholic churches have been incorporating popular music with theologically sound lyrics in rather complicated liturgical worship—often without printed materials, even in large congregations. In returning home to the U.S. and being handed huge booklets for bulletins, I sense that often we too impose foreign worship forms and music on our own folks.

Music provides a "morphology of feeling," to use a rich phrase from Suzanne

Langer,[20] giving shape to the sadness *and* the joy of the Mystery at the heart of existence. Forms of music all around us are changing, so planned or unplanned, worship is changing. Contemplative worship helps to discern contemporary music—appropriate music (traditional or modern) that expresses many cultures and contexts even in a small community. "Lord, Prepare Me to Be a Sanctuary" is a contemplative *and* contemporary hymn that can be a call for personal holiness and societal holiness—sanctuary for aliens.

Two practical options require conscious discernment: whether to bring in outside professional musicians, artists, or actors or whether to involve similarly gifted members or friends of extended church families. The Bible class teacher's young adult grandson who never attends church may be a drummer; the inactive spouse of a deacon may be an actor. Such intrafamily invitations have advantages of creating participation, reaching out to nonattending neighbors, and owning changes from within the community itself. To pay or not to pay is another issue for discernment. Even a modest payment, especially if choosing the intrafamily option, is professionally affirming and institutionally freeing.

### Complementary Worship

Complementary worship values "varieties of gifts, but the same Spirit" (1 Cor. 12:4). I would not be unhappy if it is spelled "compl*i*mentary worship," for exactly what we need is to practice complimenting one another, contemplatives and contemporaries valuing one another's gifts and traditions: "Outdo one another in showing honor" (Rom. 12:10).

Many contemporary services express great passion but lose their integrity, failing to discern if the music and rituals center on a "me and Jesus" without community. Many traditional services maintain theological integrity but have lost their passion. Complementary worship seeks to bring together passion with integrity in community.

## 3. Faith Stories—and the Worship Climate

To restore the soul of worship is to make the service a model of the contemplative interactive spiritual life. To celebrate God's work in people's lives is to make faith stories part of the fabric of the community life in all contexts, beginning with the centerpiece of worship. Such an approach to worship has implications for scripture reading, prayers and especially preaching, all traditionally more monologue than dialogue.

### Preaching and the Ministry of the Word

There are many ways to let the Word become flesh and create more interactive proclamation. Traditionally a *liturgist* is someone trained to create liturgy for the community, but today the term is often used instead of "lay reader" or "lector." I used to insist on ecclesiastically correct language, but now I say "Baptize the liturgist!" Laypeople ought to be creating liturgies to involve people! I summarize a few ways here.

- **"Baptizing" the Liturgist! (LL 7)** Many churches now use the term *liturgist* for a person who reads scripture or offers prayer. Coach your lay readers, training them to read with spirit. Create worship teams. Encourage them to pray and play until they burst into their own drama or prayers and become what they are being called—liturgists!

- **Dramatic Reading of Scriptures (LL 8)** Replace the monologue. Encourage lay readers to enlist family or church family members to read the parts of narrator and characters in the ancient story. Ask someone to mime the text as it is read. Or use a narrator-interview method with Deborah, Isaiah or Paul. (*Lectionary Scenes* provides dramatic vignettes for the church year.[21] Adapt LL 13 and Resource IV, "The Worship Interview," for biblical characters, using scripture.)

- **Pulpit Roundtable (LL 9)** Gather a small group of people to pray and converse about the scriptures for the next week's sermon. This provides a living commentary on the Word enfleshed in your unique community and makes the sermon dialogical.[22] By inviting people for six- to eight-week periods, many have the opportunity and the experience maintains vitality.

- **Pulpit Touring vs. Pulpiteering (LL 10)** The pulpit creates a barrier yet is a powerful symbol. Try beginning and ending the message in the pulpit, taking an appropriate tour in between to tell a story, ask a question, or get responses.

- **Silence—and Response after the Sermon (LL 11)** Allow for silence following the sermon. Occasionally invite brief responses, in the manner of a mini-Quaker meeting, to reflect on the sermon's connection with life (or share one-to-one in the pew as in LL 12).

St. James (Anglican) Church on Piccadilly Square, London, prints this in the bulletin:

After the preacher has finished the sermon, the congregation is invited to reflect on what has been said—either in silence or in words—as the Spirit moves. In this way, the sermon becomes a shared breaking of the Word of God. After ten minutes, the liturgy proceeds.

## Faith Sharing in Congregational Worship

For faith finding and faith sharing to be normative in church life, they must be validated in the worship setting. Methods like the "pulpit roundtable" are particularly challenging to the preacher in terms of safeguarding confidential stories; ask for permission even to share them anonymously: "As one of you reflected this past week...."

Another challenge is for leaders to use their own vulnerable experience, so essential to validate others to open up their stories; yet there is a danger of self-absorption. John Killinger was once asked if he thought it was OK for ministers to use personal stories in their sermons. He paused, then replied, "Yes, it's all right so long as the stories put the preacher in the position of needing grace." Genuine faith sharing is not from *above* but from *below*. It is a theological statement: Christ entered the low places—the manger, the cross.

- **Faith Sharing in the Pew (LL 12)** Create a brief time occasionally for faith sharing in worship. Invite people to reflect silently on a simple gift of the past week—then to share briefly with another person or two. Try this method in response to the sermon—or adapt Resource III, "Faith Finding, Faith Sharing," as a part of the sermon. OPTION: Design a question based on the sermon text (also print the question) for conversing after worship, at home, or at work. During the announcements and at the end of the sermon, announce the following: "The faith sharing question today is...."

- **The Worship Interview (LL 13)** Reinvent the "witness" or "testimony," an ancient biblical tradition. One way to validate people's ordinary faith experiences is to adapt the popular interview format, a brief three- to five-minute witness to God at work in life. The interview also can provide a fresh format to bring mission to your doorstep. (See Resource IV.)

- **Carrying the Portable Mike (LL 14)** Taking the microphone to persons who want to offer prayers, make announcements, or make responses is a service of worship so that all can hear (a possibility for a youth project).

While writing this section, I got a phone call that proved not to be an interruption. A pastor began telling me how in his church's contemporary service people sometimes offer testimonies so close to his sermon theme that he simply affirms the Spirit speaking through them, setting aside much of his prepared text. E. M. Bounds wrote, "The preacher must have had audience and ready access to God before he [or she] can have access to the people."[23] That ready access may make the minister receptive to the people's gifts.

## 4. Silences in the Service of Worship

"Words, created *by* and used *in* our conscious life, are not the essence of prayer. The essence of prayer is the act of God who is working in us and raises our whole being to [God]self," wrote theologian Paul Tillich.[24] Understood in this way, the spoken words and printed liturgies are only prompters to deeper contemplation. Marva Dawn observes,

> In hundreds of congregations I have visited in my freelancing, there have been fewer than a handful who actually spend time in silence in their worship services. The angels know better. The heavenly worship described in the Book of Revelation (Rev. 8:1) includes a mysterious half hour of silence.[25]

Fred Rogers, an ordained Presbyterian minister, prophetically broke with television protocol in *Mister Rogers' Neighborhood*, allowing silences while a child tied her shoes. Creating sabbath pauses to leaven the service is in itself a prophetic service, a countercultural witness against technology taking over the liturgies of our lives. Interpret silences as "hush times" for children. As you pause and pray you can also deal with negative feelings—about self, a worship leader, a worshiper, a crying baby—contagiously transforming the atmosphere.[26]

- Silences in the Service (LL 15) Weaving spaces in corporate liturgies makes worship a service, modeling sabbath times in the liturgies of our lives. Try leavening the service with several silent pauses in addition to one(s) that may be printed. For example:
  1. Before reading (or hearing) scripture, pause to pray silently that the Word may speak to you as you read (or hear), as well as to others.
  2. After a moving anthem, as worship leader(s), try sitting prayerfully a moment, then continue with the next part in the service.

3. Pause and pray during a sermon (to repeat a quote or phrase, to let it sink in); then afterward allow silence for people to meditate on its connections to life. Cultivate this simple practice: "Pause and pray."

✦ **The Shape of Solitude (LL 16)** Encourage one another to take half an hour for personal prayer *at least four days a week* (list next Sunday's scriptures in the bulletin), to take *at least two minutes of silence* to begin each day no matter how busy or late you are, to pray during the day, and a couple of times a year to take an overnight and day of personal retreat to pray. Shape your solitude in ways that draw you to pray to be shaped by God. (See Resource VIII, "Spiritual Wellness for Ministry.")

A deeper aspect of the discipline of solitude is to remain faithful to a community, willing to be true to your unique call while not always being understood or conforming to others' expectations.

## 5. Worship as Hospitality

The Lord's Supper dramatizes Jesus' table fellowship with outcasts, and our job is to extend the table. Saint Benedict's words might be included as instructions to ushers, pastors, lay leaders, and church members:

> Let all guests who arrive be received like Christ, for he is going to say, "I came as a guest, and you received me." And to all let due honor be shown....In the reception of the poor and of pilgrims the greatest care and solicitude should be shown, because it is especially in them that Christ is received.

Hospitality in worship takes many forms: a parking usher plan, fresh-baked bread for visitors, a community food barrel, passing the peace, name tags, friendship pads, language that includes rather than excludes, a wheel chair project for victims of land mines. In churches like St. Giles (Presbyterian) in Edinburgh, Scotland, and in St. Bartholomew's (Episcopal) in New York City, I have made my way forward to huddle around the Communion table with hundreds, joining hands for the Lord's Prayer, offering joys and concerns aloud, receiving Communion like a huge family, feeling one with the world. Intimacy need not be limited by size.

✦ **Removing Barriers to God (LL 17)** Discover the rich treasure of male and female metaphors for God in the Bible: a nursing mother

(Isa. 49:15; 66:13), a compassionate father (Ps. 103:13). Explore names for God beyond parental images: rock, sun, shield, light, water of life, fire, Holy One, shepherd, host, etc. Use them in personal, small-group, or corporate prayers.

- **Balancing the Lord's Prayer (LL 18)** Balance masculine with feminine metaphors: Precede the Lord's Prayer with a feminine biblical image: "We turn to you, O God, for like a mother eagle, you bear us on your wings and bring us to yourself. And now we pray the family prayer, Our Father...." (Or, "We turn to you, O God, for like a woman sweeping till she finds her priceless lost coin, you search for us. And now we pray....")

- **Disabilities Awareness and Access (LL 19)** Corporate hospitality for marginalized persons (*anawim* in Hebrew) creates a ripple effect of hospitality in people's homes and work. Engage with others in an awareness exercise: List the various barriers that church and nonchurch people experience. Then go beyond physical, visual, audio, and spatial barriers to speak of spiritual, emotional, musical, and linguistic barriers. Reflect together in your context.

- **Weekly Communion (LL 20)** Encourage weekly Eucharist based on its biblical, traditional, and Reformation ideal—its multisensory benefits and drama of hospitality.[27] This need not be a barrier if seekers are free to discern whether to commune or not. Consider varied methods (in the pew, coming forward, more than one location) or an option just to receive prayers. (See LL 46.)

Virtually every visitor or inactive returnee has experienced a recent crisis, so it takes real courage for them to come through your church door. With a sixth sense you begin to hear of a car crash, a recent move, a death of a loved one, a stillborn child, a career crisis, a lover's or a parent's crisis. Even a handshake or a meeting of the eyes can become a prayer. We need to train pastors, lay visitors, phone callers, ushers, and people in the pews to listen through people's Sunday appearances for the tips of these submerged crises. Such deep listening would affect our prayers, our presence, and our programs.

Today's seekers are craving to experience the three most popular lines around the world: Welcome home. I love you. Supper's ready.

# CHAPTER FOUR

# The Soul of Administration
*Contemplative Leadership*

## ROMANS 12

I appeal to you therefore, brothers and sisters, by the mercies of God, to present your bodies as a living sacrifice, holy and acceptable to God, which is your spiritual worship. Do not be conformed to this world, but be transformed by the renewing of your minds, **so that you may discern what is the will of God—what is good and acceptable and perfect.** For by the grace given to me I say to everyone among you not to think of yourself more highly than you ought to think, but to think with sober judgment, each according to the measure of faith that God has assigned. **For as in one body we have many members, and not all the members have the same function, so we, who are many, are one body in Christ, and individually we are members one of another. We have gifts that differ according to the grace given to us: prophecy, in proportion to faith; ministry, in ministering; the teacher, in teaching; the exhorter, in exhortation; the giver, in generosity; the leader, in diligence; the compassionate, in cheerfulness.** Let love be genuine; hate what is evil, hold fast to what is good; love one another with mutual affection; outdo one another in showing honor. **Do not lag in zeal, be ardent in spirit, serve the Lord.** Rejoice in hope, be patient in suffering, persevere in prayer. Contribute to the needs of the saints; extend hospitality to strangers. Bless those who persecute you; bless and do not curse them. Rejoice with those who rejoice, weep with those who weep. Live in harmony with one another; do not be haughty, but associate with the lowly; do not claim to be wiser than you are. Do not repay anyone evil for evil, but take thought for what is noble in the sight of all. If it is possible, so far as it depends on you, live peaceably with all. Beloved, never avenge yourselves, but leave room for the wrath of God; for it is written, "Vengeance is mine, I will repay, says the Lord." No, "if your enemies are hungry, feed them; if they are thirsty, give them something to drink; for by doing this you will heap burning coals on their heads." Do not be overcome by evil, but overcome evil with good.

# O Send Forth!

Kent Ira Groff, 2000
From Psalm 43:3

Kent Ira Groff, 2000

*May be sung by itself; between spoken intercessions;
or before, between, and after verses of Psalm 43.*

Text and music © Kent Ira Groff, 2000.

# The Soul of Administration
## Contemplative Leadership

*Diakonía—*
"Administering to people's needs"

What the church needs today is not more machinery or better, not new organizations or more novel methods, but people whom the Holy Spirit can use—people of prayer....The Holy Spirit does not flow through methods, but through people...and does not come on machinery, but on people...and does not anoint plans, but people—people of prayer....The Church of God makes, or is made by, its leaders.[28]

—E. M. Bounds, *Power through Prayer*

*Try this exercise as a way of praying on the job. Seat yourself at a table or desk where you normally work: paying bills, writing memos, making phone calls, conversing with fellow workers. Now gently push the chair back several inches—distancing yourself from your work. Spend a few minutes in quiet retreat—your own portable monastery. Then move forward to engage in the next task. Practice this throughout your week alone, or together with others in a meeting.*

Administration too often is viewed as an irritation that stifles the life-giving Spirit. It is viewed as less spiritual, to be given to the laity if possible, furthering the pastor-people and spiritual-secular rift, not to mention the effect on self-esteem.

Yet Stephen who was ordained to administer a nonprofit food program—not to preach the word—was "a man full of faith and the Holy Spirit." But he wove a creative tapestry and preached anyway, becoming the church's first martyr (Acts

6:5; 7:1–8:1). *Administrare*, the Latin root of administration, means "ministry to"—*diakonía* in Greek.

# 1. Discerning Vision
## The Soul of Contemplative Leadership

After gathering to respond to the good news in worship, the next step of disciples is to discern the needs of the community and the world at our doorstep: How are we being called to minister?

A key word for "leadership" (NRSV) or "administration" (RSV) is *cybernesis* in Greek—literally "piloting." As maintaining a clear vision is a pilot's job, so discernment ranks as a *spiritual gift* along with apostles and teachers! (See 1 Cor. 12:28.) It is a marvel of language that "cybernetics"—this same New Testament term for spiritual leadership—is used as a term describing today's computer revolution. We need courses in "spiritual cybernetics" for lay and clergy leaders to integrate technological and contemplative forms of administration, while keeping alive the visioning-piloting element. "Cyberspace" takes on a whole new meaning, cultivating a leadership style that values space for grace in our plans and projects, our recommendations and recruitment.

The soul of administration is developing contemplative leadership, calling forth gifts of the community essential for a given ministry situation. Five times in one chapter Paul directs the wild Corinthian community to the litmus test for discerning spiritual gifts: to excel in gifts "for building up" the community in love for love (1 Cor. 14:3, 5, 12, 17, 26; see also Eph. 4:16).

So every administrative issue, each building, financial, maintenance, or personnel decision, has one focus: How can this very process of deciding foster community-building—not just building structures and infrastructures—in this board, this body, and beyond? How does this action pilot us toward God's vision (*cybernesis*)? How will this action minister to people's needs *and* call forth gifts of the community (*administrare*)?

One thing is clear: The "more excellent way" is to weave all this administrative business with genuine love (1 Cor. 13; Rom. 12:9). The soul of administration is to cultivate contemplative leadership, weaving spiritual practices while administering to people via programs for worshiping, learning, caring, and witnessing in word and deed.

*The habit of corporate discernment in ordinary administrative meetings becomes the key to weaving this creative tapestry.*

From twenty years as a parish pastor and twelve as founder and director of a nonprofit organization, I confess this art is very difficult. I see three essentials: a vision of mission, personal and communal; a shift in corporate decision making from undue reliance on Roberts' Rules of Order to a biblical discernment process; and a shift from recruitment for jobs to discernment of gifts. I do not offer answers, only hints, because as you pray you will develop your own vision and skills in the art of communal discernment.

## A Visioning Discernment Process

The art of discernment is the beginning and end point for contemplative leadership: finding and living out of a unique vision in Christ, personally and communally. Its twin processes are *visioning* and *discerning with love* on the way toward the vision, to be modeled at all levels among staff, leaders, and members. As Robert Greenleaf put it, "This model, *because it is a thing of beauty, in itself*, becomes a powerful serving force."[29]

Without a vision the people perish. Before building programs and edifices, before dismantling or repairing them, we come back to the soul of administration: leaders engaged in prayerful planning to discern a vision—a passion for whom, how, when, and where they are called to minister. As E. M. Bounds wrote a century ago, "The Holy Spirit does not flow through methods, but through people...does not come on machinery, but on people...does not anoint plans, but people—people of prayer."[30]

The soul of administration is restored by developing leaders who contemplate God's love *and* the world's pain. Methods are only important to serve, like conduits in the desert, to transport the life-giving water to the points of need. The need must start with leaders recognizing their own vulnerabilities, along with those of their community, or else our administrations will not really minister to people. If they do not flow from the Source, they will be only spurts that go wide of the mark.

The tapestry's backside (personal habits) and the front side (communal habits) are woven simultaneously. A board where leaders are practicing "pause and pray" individually can understand when someone calls for silence to pray during the meeting. Officers who know the value of personal retreat recognize the value of a spiritual retreat for the board.

> ◦ **Personal Spiritual Disciplines (LL 21)** Examine personal and communal *benefits* of your own disciplines of prayer: discerning your life mission; story listening, storytelling; silences to cultivate the

Presence; and hospitality to self and others. Do you perceive an integrity of soul: body, mind, spirit? What are the *barriers* to honest-to-God prayer? And what are the *bridges* to authentic prayer, methods that work for you and are suited to your personality? Pray for openness to new ways of praying for yourself, for your faith community. (See Resource VIII, "Spiritual Wellness for Ministry.")

Frederick Buechner defines the passion for an individual or a corporate mission: "The place God calls you to is the place where your deep gladness and the world's deep hunger meet."[31] That place is different for a Mozart or a Mother Teresa, for an aging downtown church or new church planting. As I write this on Labor Day 1999, National Public Radio reports that Americans work longer hours than people in any industrialized nation. But what are we working *for?*

↝ **Personal Life Mission Statement (LL 22)** Enter in your journal: *What is my purpose for being on this earth?*[32] "If your eye is single, your whole body will be full of light: (Matt. 6:22, AT).[33] Your mission is unique to you yet blesses the universe. Here are some hints: What puts a sparkle in your eyes—your deep gladness? And what pulls at your heartstrings—some hunger of the world? Avoid being too general (to glorify God) or too specific (to play the piano). Yet put your flesh on your mission: to glorify God *through* the song of your life in a way that speaks to working years or retirement or even disability. Rework your mission and keep it short; repeat it as a prayer of your heart; put it on a card inside your closet or desk or in your wallet.

Individuals who draw passion from a personal life mission can also value lifting up the congregation's vision of mission while discussing the access ramp, the leaking roof, or the newly arrived refugees.

We need to couple the habit of discernment with detachment: *the willingness to let go of our favorite plans or projects, to be open to the Spirit's "new thing" among us* (Isa. 42:9; 43:19; 48:6). It is impossible to practice corporate discernment (what is best for all) unless members are encouraged to practice personal discernment (what is best for each in relation to the community).

We can see this radical discernment with detachment in Jesus' encounter with the Canaanite woman. Jesus emptied himself of the official job description ("I was sent only to the lost sheep of the house of Israel"), ignored the disciples' advice ("Send her away)," and stayed engaged with her. Listening with one ear to a "dogged" woman's cry and with the other to Abba's divine cry, Jesus boldly chose to step across the boundary line into the territory of the marginalized, validating her faithful soul—and his own. (See Matt. 15:21-28.)

### DOGGED FAITH

The seeing eye of dogged faith
shall triumph over human schemes:
I shall make plans,
give up my plans.

—Kent Ira Groff © 1998

The process of forming or reforming a corporate vision rests on and tests the willingness of individuals or small groups within the large group to say to one another and God simultaneously, "I will make plans, give up my plans."

"A simple habit of spirit and a holy but humble indifference to all consequences," as Richard Cecil put it two centuries ago, highlights the countercultural tension between administering Christ's corporation and managing Wall Street's corporation. Holiness then is a simple habit of detachment or spiritual neutrality: "a holy but humble indifference to all consequences." Ignatius of Loyola would tell us patience and courage are required, and a spiritual retreat is a good place to begin rehearsing.

- **Spiritual Leadership Retreat (LL 23)** Merely a church calendar announcement that church leaders are at prayer is a powerful form of leadership, a witness to the value of silence and contemplation. Try a "fasting and prayer" leadership retreat or portion of one (a common Korean practice) dedicated to growing in spiritual depth or in breadth of compassion for certain groups. (Or try a juice and fruit fast.) The retreat might focus on a visioning process or incorporating contemplative practices in the business meetings.

One of the most helpful ways of going about the visioning process is a retreat, which best begins with the aid of an outside facilitator trained in contemplative practices *and* organizational planning skills.

- **Corporate Visioning Process (LL 24)** One of the best beginning methods for corporate visioning and follow-through is the group *lectio divina*—prayerful reading of scripture, taking notes of images or metaphors of each person's response to texts, and listening to paradigm stories in the context of community. List participants' images (for example, tree of life, rock, water, well, body of Christ, burning bush, cornerstone) and stories. (See Resource II, "Scripture Sharing.")

- **Vision Follow-Through (LL 25)** Keep the visioning process going in regular board meetings for several months with your own leaders trained by the facilitator or with the facilitator. Let the Word become flesh, as shared biblical images can begin to meld and mold personal and denominational tradition: What in this council or board is life-giving? What is life-draining? personally? communally? Create worship experiences to lift up these concerns. Finally the facilitator may be called in again to help draft a simple vision statement, discerned from single-sentence nominations submitted by participants.

Then the task is to keep the process life-giving: Portray it on a banner. Flesh it out with specific mission strategies year by year. Consider writing a screenplay or brief story of your community's life ten years into the future.

Beware: A beautifully framed vision statement may get in the way of vision follow-through. I know a church where people would say that the mission of that church is to be a community for the sake of the world. This mission is not written; it is just in the air. It guides them in the rough and tumble of financial crisis, debates over a homeless shelter vs. programs for their own youth. I am convinced that merely the quest for a vision, plumbing the scriptures and one another's experience of God with openness to the world, is itself transformative—even if no official statement emerges. Merely the intent to pray is already prayer, in the language of the mystics.

## An Atmosphere of Discernment: Beyond Robert's Rules

Discernment affects our mode of corporate decision making. Words often sound like what they do: *decide* cuts off, focuses on *product; discern* opens up, focuses on *process.* Paul pleads, "Present your bodies as a living sacrifice.... be transformed by the renewing of your minds, so that you may *discern what is the will of God*" (Rom. 12:1-2, emphasis added). Detachment is the personal sacrifice that creates space for communal discernment.

The New Testament uses two Greek words for discernment interchangeably: *dokimé,* "testing, ringing true"; and *diakrisis,* "through crisis" or "judging through." Discernment means "testing through crisis." Many church bodies are good at information and actual deciding but need help in building the spiritual fabric of community while getting there so the decision has spiritual ownership and depth. Wise decisions are the ripened fruit of a discernment process.

Most denominations have adapted some form of democratic process in their administrative life. But "modern" (only century-old) *Robert's Rules of Order* and denominational policy manuals often leave little room for the Spirit in discerning the far more ancient balancing of scripture, tradition, reason, and experience.[34] Parliamentary procedure was made for community, not vice versa, and it can be used rather minimally if we focus on transforming community (Rom. 12:2).

A prayerful process that begins with self-examination and ends with what Quakers call "the sense of the meeting" is more true to scripture than a majority wins mind-set that degenerates into acquiescing and feeling sabotaged. "Let each person examine oneself"—while examining, drawing from, and seeking the good of the community: "For all who eat and drink without discerning the body judge themselves" (1 Cor. 11:28-29, AT). Actually breaking bread during a church administrative meeting can foster this tone of self-examined community discernment.

Romans 12 calls us to discern—*in a way that transforms us*—what is the intention of God in our time on a host of volatile issues: sexuality and scripture, poverty and peace. These very issues can be the occasion for a corporate discernment process which, wedded to representative government, could itself be God's great gift for the post-Constantinian church and world!

Discernment does include healthy debate: The presbyters in Acts 15 had their say on an issue so volatile it threatened the future of the church (vv. 2, 7). Quakers call this stage of discernment "release"—*prayerfully saying your truth and being heard.* Then comes the key: "The whole assembly kept silence, and listened" (15:12). We see the fruit of this early church council: "For it has seemed good to the Holy Spirit and to us to impose on you no further burden than these essentials" (15:28). They reached *the sense of the meeting*—a new place in God where a solution beyond human plans awaits the community, confirmed by silence.

❧ **Beyond *Robert's Rules*** (LL 26) Pray for your church to engage in a Spirit-led, biblically grounded discernment process for reforming Christ's body in its governing bodies and boards from national to local levels. The purpose is twofold:

1. Develop the discernment process to create and renew its vision of Christ's mission.

2. Cultivate an ethos of discernment to leaven the community's ongoing decision-making proceedings.

The *process* of discernment could outlive any visions or decisions, transforming our win-lose way of "doing church" in the twenty-first century into "being church" as we are formed around the pattern of the self-emptying Messiah, who rises again and again in contemplative communities of obedient disciples (Phil. 2:1-11).

### *Recruitment for Jobs vs. Discernment of Gifts*

Discernment as the heart of administration involves a movement from an organizational mode of recruitment to do a job to an organic mode of discerning the gifts, purpose, and passion of the members. It is a call to live out the organic metaphor described in 1 Corinthians 12–14 and Romans 12 that we are Christ's body, and each member is endowed with a manifestation of the Spirit for the common good; that discerning the will of God is all about ministering to one another and the world by developing our unique gifts in community.

Churches generally relegate this recruitment to a nominating committee and pastor who diligently recruit people to fill the necessary slots. These suggestions are not designed to do an end run around local or denominational policy manuals but to advocate Jesus' approach to tradition: "The sabbath was made for humankind, and not humankind for the sabbath" (Mark 2:27; see also Mark 7:1-30).

> **Gifts Discernment Team (LL 27)** If a core of members is in touch with its passion and life mission, church ministries can be redesigned interactively around the gifts of the body, and the nominating committee becomes the Gifts Discernment Team. (See also LL 22, "Personal Life Mission Statement.")

## 2. Community Faith Stories in Administration

Denominational polity held the pastor responsible for seeing that persons chaired the major committees of the congregation. But no one in St. Matthew's seemed right to chair the stewardship committee. Rather than recruit someone just to fill a slot, the pastor was given the blessing of the council to leave the position vacant while they engaged in prayer. Time was running out when during a late summer work project a new member engaged the pastor in a discussion about why there was little mention of tithing in this parish. The pastor shared the new member's concerns with the council, and eventually this young member accepted the position of stewardship chair. St. Matthew's stewardship program later became a model for the district, and the young man has now created a team to train other congregations.

Administration is all about discerning a community's gifts and resources for the sake of the world, and the bond that creates Christian community is story. Often a church will have a foundational story that acts as a hologram, reflecting the church's identity and mission, such as the one above, and below.

When Harry Vawter, a business executive, joined New Hope church, he was not asked to be on the finance committee, as in previous churches. Instead, Harry was invited to become a lay minister of a small group. He took the challenge—enjoying frontline people ministry. Five years later, when Harry died from a fast-growing brain tumor, fifteen hundred people attended his funeral. Many testified that much of what made Harry's life worthwhile consisted of the life changes he witnessed through leading a small group.[35]

A key to discerning leadership is to create space in all contexts of the community, including committee meetings, to hear one another's stories of faith. In stories we hear the edge of excitement in an engineer's voice, revealing her real passion; in stories leaders hear of risk-taking love that inspires sacrifice for the common good, "which is your spiritual worship" (Rom. 12:1).

## Spirituality Matters for Committee Meetings

Nothing is more vital to the soul of the postmodern church than leavening business meetings with relationships to build community, to inspire service. Literature on growing churches is consistent: with or without walls, privileged in the northern hemisphere or persecuted in the southern hemisphere. Churches that grow missionally, spiritually, and numerically place a high value on small groups. "High-tech, high-touch": The expression illustrates that people depersonalized by technology crave intimacy and individuality.

Here is the church's opportunity! Yet in a fast-paced world, many people do not take time to participate in a growth group in addition to the basics of Sunday morning and serving on church and community committees. The church copies culture, leaving little space for vulnerability to share our hurts and joys, especially in its "showcase" of corporate worship and certainly not in its many task-oriented committees.

### Recognize the Barriers

We find a new church member, often dealing with a fresh life crisis, recruited by the finance committee serving with the long-term member who is a good accountant but unaware of the other's spiritual needs. Both may actually be "young" spiritually. They have a vague yearning for spiritual conversation, yet it is not likely to happen here for several reasons:

❖ It is scary to be vulnerable with little feeling in common except the committee.

❖ It is not natural in agenda-centered meetings to bare your soul.

❖ Committees have a task, so folks fear "relationship" time will kidnap the agenda.

Yet we disown the soul of church whenever we repair the ecclesiastical machinery without pausing to celebrate God's work in people's lives. *Doing church without being church for one another is a theological oxymoron!*

In a denominational committee on which I served, I was aware that one person's father had been diagnosed with cancer; the child of a minister was in a major medical center with a life-threatening crisis; one was leaving her job; another had just placed a parent in a nursing home; my daughter was dealing with anorexia; and a colleague had just had a book accepted for publication. The traditional "before" and "after" prayers were offered, but this allowed no space to name these personal concerns to one another and God.

It is not that we were "bad" disciples but that life is complex. Logically there was *not* time to express all these needs. Yet those bearing the concerns had no opportunity to unburden—enough to make them vote no on a major motion! Most members went away not knowing and unable to pray for others' needs. For Christians to gather to *do* the church's work yet not *be* the church breeds a low-grade, corporate dis-ease. No wonder there is so much conflict! How can leaders pray with and for the people yet not care for one another?

We need new models that recognize the constraints of time, the dynamics of larger churches and of smaller family-style churches where intimacy is assumed. How can we provide a safe, brief way to "bear one another's burdens, and in this way fulfill the law of Christ" (Gal.6:2)? The only way out of our addiction to "business as usual" is to have group ownership for the agenda and to include both organic *and* organizational development—spirituality *and* productivity.

## Raise the Crucial Question

You need commitment from those involved. Leaders can use conversations and classes, worship cues or sermons to raise urgent issues. Use brief stories of your own to model the process of being church to one another. A pastor may assume lay leaders will not support such changes, and a member may assume the same of the pastor. Either way, start by raising questions:

❖ How can we become servant-leaders to one another in our needs?

❖ How can our meetings model the pattern for genuine community?

❖ Will we as servant-leaders devote some ratio of time in our business meetings to *being* church as well as *doing* church?

The last point is crucial: to set aside intentional time (fifteen to twenty minutes) in each meeting to nurture communal life with God and a prayerful agenda.

## Lift Up the Benefits

This model of administration benefits relationships *and* task. Not only will it enhance the group as community; it will also have a positive effect on the quality of the group decisions. If you as a layperson or pastor believe this, find a way to say so. Others will likely give it a try.

Being church for one another has advantages for large and small congregations. Large churches need this to keep them caring and attentive to individuals. First Presbyterian Church, Bethlehem, Pennsylvania, has been using an approach like this for decades. Members who move away to another community say, "I just can't find another church that is so intimate and caring." Yet it has three thousand members!

In small and average-sized churches, much of the conflict comes from an unspoken fear that too many "new folks" will break down the close sense of family. So this model can help the smaller church become more inviting and not fear growth. Increased numbers need *not* make the church less personal as long as it provides safe places for caring.

I have often found myself misspelling the words *mediation* and *meditation*. Somewhere along the way it occurred to me that my little mind-trick contained a message. There is a close connection between the arts of meditation and mediation: Witness how often psalms full of contention call the community to meditate on the law of love. (See Psalm 119.)

An Episcopal minister tells how colleagues ask if his vestry meetings are contentious. He proceeds to describe how he leads a contemplative Bible study with his vestry, choosing a scripture that fits with key issues on the agenda that month, asking questions like, "How is this text speaking to you, to All Saints Church, right here?" "It's incredibly renewing," he comments, "and it's hard to be contentious with someone after you've opened the same Bible and prayed together." (See Resource II, "Scripture Sharing.")

Here is the model: Open each meeting with time to be present to God and to one another, but a key is to invite people to some time of sharing *one-to-one* (or in very small groups). This kind of sharing is safer for the introvert, keeps extroverts from dominating, saves time, and over time fosters several deepening relationships. Spiritual building and bonding takes place in many ways. Listen to one another's experiences of grit and grace and encourage brief faith vignettes as part of committee reports. This sharing links the church's stories with the divine story. The actions of the meeting will more likely spring from the well of contemplation and silence.

> ➵ **The Meeting of Persons (LL 28)** This one single practice of fostering intentional space in every meeting for the meeting of persons with God and one another can revolutionize the church by making it a model of community. After leading a guided meditation, posing a question for reflection, or praying silently with scripture, invite each to share concerns with a person on his or her left or right. Following six to ten minutes meeting in dyads, some of those concerns may be shared with the whole group in a time of prayer—or between verses of a hymn or chant sung as a prayer. Use or adapt exercises like LL 38, "An Examen of Consciousness." (See also Resource V, "Space for Grace in the Agenda.")

## 3. Silences: Space for Grace in the Agenda

In a church I served, four persons fainted in worship over a two-year period, two in the early service and two in the later service. Since I did not know in those days how to be still and contemplate, it never occurred to me to invite our worship committee and session to contemplate in silence, to listen beneath these outward events. A query such as, What might the Spirit be trying to say to us through these repeated experiences? could have paid immeasurable dividends. (The deacons did listen and started a CPR training program that became a blessing to the health of the congregation.) Silence in community might have surfaced deeper insights, revealing other rumblings in the system. Scores of new folks were joining, oldsters were feeling anxious in this historic 1740 "meetinghouse"—squeezed in behind little doors on the pews. The unnamed demon of too much church growth, homesteaders threatening pioneers, could have surfaced in a prayerful atmosphere instead of blowing up a year later. It also might have surfaced that there was no ventilation system to temper the stifling meetinghouse with a bit of fresh air.

Below are some exercises that invite a prayerful approach for church boards and committees or denominational conferences.

- **Contemplative Intercessory Prayer (LL 29)** Learning to listen with God and one another is essential for cultivating silences in the meetings of persons and in the agenda. Invite the group to begin to pray silently, as if God is speaking: "Be still...and know that I am God" (Ps. 46:10). Allow concerns to surface within, repeating the prayer, then letting go of words in silence. End by inviting concerns to be named aloud, repeating the text as a litany between each personal, church, and world concern.

- **Leavening the Agenda (LL 30)** The goal is to weave the agenda with spaces to be aware of the Presence. Try some of these suggestions: schedule short times on the docket for a chant or a spiritual song, reading a scripture, a unison prayer—followed by silence; or invite persons to stay or leave the room for a brief "retreat" in a nearby chapel or outdoors and then return at a certain time. And adopt an agreed-upon practice that anyone may spontaneously call for silence. *Intra*personal intelligence enriches *inter*personal intelligence. (See Resource V, "Space for Grace in the Agenda.")

- **Passing the Chalice—or the Font (LL 31)** Open the meeting with an empty Communion chalice from your church (or from a congregation in a denominational conference) placed before the group with appropriate scripture, hymn, or prayer. Mention that during the business agenda the empty chalice will be passed prayerfully throughout the group as a sign of mutual ministry. (Adapt by using a baptismal font and towel, art work, or a clergy stole. See Resource V, "Space for Grace in the Agenda.")

## 4. Hospitality in Administration

The connection of administration with people's accessibility needs is obvious—kinesthetic and spatial hospitality extended through access ramps, parking ushers, sound systems, copiers to produce large-print bulletins. What is not so obvious is the kind of deeper listening cultivated by the practices of contemplative stories and prayer.

Prayer begins by paying attention—to a haunting phrase in scripture or in a lunch conversation, a fragment of a dream, an irritating occurrence in a family or church family system. A Church of the Brethren congregation tells this story. The phrase "no room in the inn" began to speak to their wellness team. They noticed a twelve-year-old child in a wheel chair, a woman with multiple sclerosis, a man with one leg.

> *No room in the inn.* No money. No leadership. No commitment. Many stairs, which, for [people with disabilities], meant there was no room for them in the inn....An elevator for the church building was impossible, they said. They talked about it and rejected it again and again.
>
> Then Lafiya came to the church. [Lafiya is a Church of the Brethren program, based on a Nigerian model, named for a Hausa word meaning "well being."] It opened our eyes to the people around us. We shared each others' stories. No longer were the questions of money or leadership the most important. Now we looked at the twelve-year-old boy in the wheelchair and wondered what it felt like to be carried up and down the stairs to Sunday school and fellowship activities. Now we looked at the woman with multiple sclerosis and asked how much she missed by not being able to go down the stairs to celebrate the Lord's Supper. Now we looked in the eyes of the man with one leg and said, "We cannot listen to your needs without responding."
>
> Soon we had the elevator, along with handicapped-accessible lavatories, a ramp and a covered entryway, and a new area for after-worship fellowship. Just before Christmas, we gathered while the boy, the woman, and the man cut the ribbon across the elevator door and rode to the fellowship hall. Now they had found room in our church, but more importantly, they had found room in our hearts.[36]

## 5. Prayer and Awareness in Church Business

A pastor tells of entering on a weekday afternoon the room where the church board would meet that night to vote on a controversial building program that could split the church. Chair by chair he sat down, visualizing and praying for each elder. (These were Presbyterians, so he was sure where each would sit in this session meeting!) For over an hour he prayed in solitude, while at the same time being in community with them. During that night's meeting, he sensed an amazing quality of Presence—with concern for the building in relation to the people and the world. (See LL 32.)

Once I was preparing notes for a seminary committee for which I was responsible. But as I pondered the people who would be coming, I began thinking about distances they would drive, contexts of their workplaces, their personal agendas for being on this committee—aware of a few names I hardly knew. Putting aside my notes, I spent about twenty minutes visualizing each in the above contexts. It was then time to leave for the meeting. As the members arrived, I felt I had already met them! The agenda seemed to flow with a spirit of unity and risk taking.

These stories make another important point: We need not only to schedule times for prayer but also to open ourselves to let prayer happen. Opening ourselves to prayer can change what we think we know and make us more aware of needing one another's insights. A woman recounted how another report had been given that the roof was leaking again, like an annual ritual. She spoke up: Had anyone checked the basement? The others, all men as it happened, dismissed her. It was, after all, the *roof* that was leaking, which clearly had to be fixed. Later one member said he thought she might be onto something; he would pay for a professional evaluation. As it turned out, the basement pilasters and joists had in fact disintegrated, causing the annual roof problems. The story shows the value of a contemplative and holistic attitude even when dealing with property maintenance issues, and also underscores the value of masculine and feminine insights in community life.

**Praying for Board Members (LL 32)** You can pray in community while in solitude. Try one of these methods: Go into the room where your board or committee meets. Chair by chair, sit for a few minutes, visualizing and praying for each member. Another option is to take a list of board members, sit quietly without words, and simply visualize each face. Or glance prayerfully over a list, put it down, close your eyes, and see which members come to you, being present to them as you are drawn.

As an experiment, a church conflict consultant arranged for a group to be in prayer down the hall while he met with the "warring" factions of a congregation. He noticed such a change in the normally turbulent atmosphere that it is now part of his standard consulting procedures to ask such a group to be convened during conflict consultations. What if such a practice were used as preventive maintenance, as we do on our automobiles? What would happen if a group or an hourly vigil were convened to be in prayer during *every* monthly church board meeting or committee nights?

**Vigil during a Board Meeting (LL 33)** Ask an existing or new group to convene in the building to pray for the church and its leaders while the board meets. Or plan a prayer vigil (with sign-in times) to meet in prayer during every monthly church board meeting or committee night. Provide the group with resources for singing, praying with scripture and specific board concerns, as well as pastoral needs. (Note: Research shows that vigils draw more men to prayer than do typical, conversational prayer groups.[37])

### Complex and Contemplative

Practice "pause and pray" during the agendas of private life and public meetings. Prayer, the utterly simple rest between two notes in discord, plays itself out in complex, contemplative decisions. It is like breathing, which appears so simple for the complex human body. Yet this is no mechanical view of prayer. We are not praying to have a conflict-free or a successful organization. Rather, we pray to be the organic presence of Christ in the world—light, salt, yeast—allowing love to permeate the simplest and the most complex action. In Mother Teresa's words, "We can do no great things, only small things with great love."

## CHAPTER FIVE

# The Soul of Education
## *Faith Stories*

**ROMANS 12**

I appeal to you therefore, brothers and sisters, by the mercies of God, to present your bodies as a living sacrifice, holy and acceptable to God, which is your spiritual worship. **Do not be conformed to this world, but be transformed by the renewing of your minds, so that you may discern what is the will of God—what is good and acceptable and perfect. For by the grace given to me I say to everyone among you not to think of yourself more highly than you ought to think, but to think with sober judgment, each according to the measure of faith that God has assigned.** For as in one body we have many members, and not all the members have the same function, so we, who are many, are one body in Christ, and individually we are members one of another. We have gifts that differ according to the grace given to us: prophecy, in proportion to faith; ministry, in ministering; **the teacher, in teaching;** the exhorter, in exhortation; the giver, in generosity; the leader, in diligence; the compassionate, in cheerfulness. Let love be genuine; hate what is evil, hold fast to what is good; love one another with mutual affection; outdo one another in showing honor. Do not lag in zeal, be ardent in spirit, serve the Lord. Rejoice in hope, be patient in suffering, persevere in prayer. Contribute to the needs of the saints; extend hospitality to strangers. Bless those who persecute you; bless and do not curse them. Rejoice with those who rejoice, weep with those who weep. Live in harmony with one another; do not be haughty, but associate with the lowly; **do not claim to be wiser than you are. Do not repay anyone evil for evil, but take thought for what is noble in the sight of all.** If it is possible, so far as it depends on you, live peaceably with all. Beloved, never avenge yourselves, but leave room for the wrath of God; for it is written, "Vengeance is mine, I will repay, says the Lord." No, "if your enemies are hungry, feed them; if they are thirsty, give them something to drink; for by doing this you will heap burning coals on their heads." Do not be overcome by evil, but overcome evil with good.

# For God Alone

Kent Ira Groff, 1996
From Psalm 62:1

Traditional Pentatonic Chant
Arr. Kent Ira Groff, 1996

*May be sung by itself; between spoken intercessions;*
*or before, between, or after verses of Psalm 62.*

# The Soul of Education
## Faith Stories

*Didaché—*
"Teaching by stories, questions, repetition, and
example"

The great vocation of the minister is to continuously make
connections between human story and the divine story.

—Henri J. M. Nouwen, The Living Reminder

We come across two types of education—the domesticating
education and the liberating education....As against this
domesticating education, liberating education aims at liberating
people....Such a liberating education is to be participatory
education where the educators and the learners work together.

—Gnana Robinson, Deeper Spirituality

The heart has its reasons which reason knows nothing of.

—Blaise Pascal, Pensées

There are so many stories,
more beautiful than answers.

—Mary Oliver, House of Light

*Take a few minutes to pray. Center yourself. Ask for new ways to
learn. Then listen to the stories of your own life as you read, as you
connect with the stories of others in your community and with the
divine story.*

The soul of education is to move from *in*formation to a holistic process of *re*formation, integrating heart and mind. It is the whole person being formed and re-formed, like a potter shaping the clay, incorporating the integrity, passion, and wholeness of Christ.

### *"Teach Us to Pray": The Education of Desire*

"The devastating separation of spirituality and theology...must be undone.... And spiritual practices, linked to both feeling and form, are the key to what we, students and teachers alike, presume to hear as our calling: education as formation," writes David Tracy. He hopes for "a slow shift of our attachments, a painstaking education of desire—an education like that which Plato foresaw as our best, and perhaps our only hope for both living and thinking well."[38] The education of desire is what "leavening the liturgies" is all about.

Catholics use "spiritual formation" as a term for Christian education, the root meaning of the Protestant "Re-formation": the form of the dying-rising Lord shaping the organic, pulsating body of Christ and each of its members.

Spiritual formation is a movement from hearing the gospel story to being part of the story ourselves, continuing "all that Jesus began to do and teach" (Acts 1:1, RSV). It is apprenticing with the Servant Lord in the joys, the conflicts, the sufferings, and the wonder portrayed in the Gospels: "Take my yoke upon you, and learn from me" (Matt. 11:29). This pattern of the emptying-rising Christ is the soul of education: "Let the same mind be in you that was in Christ Jesus, who...emptied himself" (Phil. 2:5-7).

Every genuine learning encounter creates an emptying of one's preconceived ideas, some confusion along the way toward a new insight or toward deepening intimacy with God, self, others, or world. Jesus' parables create a mini-trance: "I have said these things to you in figures of speech" (John 16:25). Genuine education is true to its origin (*educare* in Latin): "leading out" from a limiting perspective to Easter horizons, from enslavement to empowerment. *Christian* education is a process of internalizing these rhythms of grace mirrored in baptism.

From the pattern of Jesus in the Gospels we find four keys to the soul of learning. The first two are *stories* and *questions*, which, like a weaver's shuttle, form the essence of the master Teacher's method. The parable of the Good Samaritan is woven with questions from beginning ("What must I do...?" "What is written...?" "What do you read...?") to end ("Which of these three, do you think, was a neighbor?"). Third, the shuttle itself is encased in *repeatable pithy wisdom sayings*: "Go and do likewise" (Luke 10:25-37). Jesus' repetition of memorizable wisdom sayings, so common in oral cultures, is relevant to postmodern "sound-byte" culture, an equally fertile point of connection between young seekers and older adults. Hence the value of repeated choruses and chants, quotable phrases and poetry and pithy stories. Brief yet unified segments cultivate the education of desire in teaching and preaching. Like movements of a shuttle, repetition also happens in the liturgies of our lives and institutions as repeated themes reemerge. Fourth, surrounding all our learning is the teaching frame of *the example of the lived life*: "My life is my message," in words attributed to Gandhi. It is Søren Kierkegaard's deeper meaning of repetition, the congruent life where deeds match words.

*Example is the curriculum of integrity—faith that is more caught than taught.* Like gospel parables, our own faith stories are bracketed by faith questions: a quest to link the Jesus of history with the Christ of experience. We now explore these themes.

# 1. Faith Stories
## Multiple Intelligences Converge

As we weave this tapestry, learning occurs in the intersection of the warp and the weft: celebrating in worship, working in committees, caring for one another, and reaching out across cultures all become formal or informal "classrooms." The theory of multiple intelligences provides a frame for this tapestry to restore the soul of education in all eight learning modes through our life narratives. (See Interlude.)

Research shows that conceptual, technical information stimulates the left sphere of the brain. Art, music, and poetry stimulate the right sphere. However, stories stimulate both spheres. Stories are linguistic vehicles for transmitting life. They contain a story line employing sequential logic; they create imagination and space and often contain songs—or are easily adapted as musicals or ballads. Storytelling is kinesthetic by nature, creating external movement, interpersonal response, and intrapersonal movement in the hearer. Stories reflect patterns in nature: devastation and renewal, violence and beauty.

The gospel story of Jesus is the paradigm: our conflicts and celebrations in these eight learning modes converge in the one life of the crucified-rising Messiah. The repeated cycle of the Christian year reminds us that the risen Messiah continues to join us in our human journey.

 ◆ **Workshop Rotation Church School (LL 34)** This one-room schoolhouse style of education recognizes 1. the primacy of a few key biblical stories; 2. multiple modes of student and teacher learning—drama, music, nature, poetry, journaling, or multimedia; and 3. the reality of in-and-out attendance patterns. Using a Bible story per month exposes a child to the same story more than once, with different learning options.[39]

This rotation method is ideally suited for seeing oneself as part of the divine story. Here is a challenge: to use rotation learning in a way that fosters contemplative learning, with enjoyment and involvement.

Education is story from beginning to end, relating one's unique story with the universal story: "God so loved the *world*...that *whoever* believes...." (John 3:16, RSV). As Eugene Peterson writes, "Liturgy keeps us in touch with the story as it defines and shapes our beginnings and ends, our living and dying, our rebirths and blessing in this text-formed community visible and invisible....It is all story."[40]

Contemplative learning happens through cultivating a fundamental attitude to pause and wonder amid one's personal, family, and community stories, both ancient and modern. What makes faith stories different from any stories? To paraphrase Shakespeare, "The story's the thing / wherein we'll disclose the consciousness of the king"[41]—or of the queen who lives orphaned on today's streets, not realizing that each is actually an inheritor of royalty! As Pascal noted, our misery is that of deposed royalty, and the Christ of the gospel gives us back our royal heritage.

 ◆ **Faith Finding, Faith Sharing (LL 35)** Meditate on a recent obstacle in your life. Then ponder: *How did my faith, or prayer, or the community of faith, or God make a difference in my response?* Use your journal; then find a context to share. Try using this exercise to begin a committee or small-group meeting. (See Resource III.)

Faith finding and faith sharing are the golden thread that honors the dignity of our participant-teachers. Anton Boisen, who out of his own tragic mental illness founded Clinical Pastoral Education for hospital ministry, said that more people are "living human documents." We are privileged to listen contemplatively for the texts and textures of our own and others' sacred stories.

In his turbulent teens my son used to pick up *Guideposts* magazine, left helter-skelter in the family room or the bathroom, and read its pithy stories.

I discovered why. *Guideposts'* articles follow this format: life is moving along, then comes a point of crisis, a sharp downturn, followed by how the writer's faith made a difference.

To nurture faith stories is a discipline that will require sacrifice by leaders and members in the heart of the church's life: in public worship and in its many administrative meetings. Is this discipline too great a sacrifice to ask the generations to make on behalf of one another? The psalm writer defines the mission of teaching:

> Give ear, O my people, to my teaching;
> > incline your ears to the words of my mouth.
> I will open my mouth in a parable;
> > I will utter dark sayings from of old,
> things that we have heard and known,
> > that our ancestors have told us.
> We will not hide them from their children;
> > we will tell to the coming generation
> the glorious deeds of the Lord,
> > and [God's] might,
> and the wonders that [God] has done.
>
> —Psalm 78:1-4

The young generation resists answers. But by having the vulnerable courage to "utter dark sayings" out of the closets of personal family tragedies or church family testings, we will find the most power-filled action of grace. "I will open my mouth in a parable" (*mashal* in Hebrew). These dark sayings of old retold *now* create fresh paradigms to connect with youth—*and* aging generations. "There are so many stories, / more beautiful than answers," writes Mary Oliver in *House of Light.*

Wade Clark Roof, author of *A Generation of Seekers: The Spiritual Journeys of the Baby Boom Generation,* writes about why America's 80 million-strong youthful generation "may be losing its religion but finding its soul": "The vast majority don't find the traditional language meaningful. They feel there is a discrepancy or cultural lag between institutions and their personal concerns."[42] Will churches tap this hunger and close the gap?

A retired Ph.D. father told me how, over lunch, he had opened himself to his unemployed Ph.D. son, telling for the first time of a dark time of joblessness in the father's own life. Such vulnerable courage often comes as "grace under pressure," to use journalist Dorothy Parker's memorable phrase.

We need safe places to rehearse the art of storying and restorying our lives, thereby restoring the soul of church. Church is the place for healing *stories*, for healing one another's broken narratives and interrupted scripts. And church is the place for *healing* stories, which contain inklings of grace in the Greater Story. Faith stories become the norm in community—and in personal life through using a journal, expressing pain and joy in God's presence, or longing for the presence.

I mean "faith stories" as a noun *and* as a verb: faith "stories" our lives, layering them with storeys, levels of meaning; and faith stories our communities, building storeys, tiers of purpose into our corporate histories. An atmosphere of narrativity is the cradle for nativity, where Christ can be born in us today.

### STORIED TRUTH

To cradle a new insight or give
birth to any thing ever lasting:
*wrap your truth in stories.*

—Kent Ira Groff © 1998

## Education in the Liturgies of Life

A liberating education is not circumscribed to square church school classrooms. "Liturgy and learning have been linked since the birth of the Christian era, but of late they have become estranged....Religious educators and liturgists have gone their separate ways," write John Westerhoff and Gwen Kennedy Neville in *Learning Through Liturgy*.[43]

In Eastern Orthodoxy, education takes place in liturgy, permeated with words of scriptures and kinesthetic, spatial, and musical participation: kissing icons, encircling the church, smelling incense, making the sign of the cross—and silences. People stand for hours, worshiping, learning, serving. Still in places like Russia and India there may be no chairs; worshipers stand or sit on cushions. One may feel stiff, but it keeps a person attentive! Writes William Willimon: "Liturgy *is* education. The question before us ...is not *whether* our people will learn when they worship. The question is, *What* will they learn when we lead them in worship?"[44] Will they learn that Christ is incarnate in all of life?

    ~ **Assessing Corporate Worship (LL 36)** Gather others and use the eight multiple intelligences to assess how your church's worship relates to the whole person and to persons of varied ages and learning styles. (See Interlude.)

- **Assessing Personal Prayer (LL 37)** Reflect on your personal practices of contemplation, intercession, praise, scripture, readings, music, journaling, and physical movement in light of the eight multiple intelligences. (See Interlude.)

What do we teach by the liturgies of our lives? In cross-cultural ventures, outreach becomes education when our assumptions get turned upside down. "The education of desire" happens in administration when one's ego gets pruned in a board meeting—or in the fellowship time after worship, illustrated by the following story.

## 2. Faith Questions: Presence out of Emptiness

While leading a series of Sunday morning workshops for a congregation, I attended worship at the same church. I noticed a row of youth sitting together, one young man wearing a baseball cap. I like to see young people in worship and am pretty broad-minded, yet a thought went through my mind: Why is that guy trying to make a statement? Afterward at the fellowship time, I observed him quickly repositioning the cap on his bare scalp, then I recalled his story. This was Chris—and I had actually been praying for him. He had sustained a closed head injury from a car crash and was undergoing multiple surgeries. In a moment my judgmental mind-set was turned upside down: We must be born again…and again…. These are moments of reconversion, of unknowing, of valuing emptiness.

Creativity comes not from trying to know but in moments of unknowing. "The earth was a formless void": Then came the moment of creation (Gen. 1:2). Spiritual creativity has to do with valuing apparent waste: pauses in conversation; margins on pages; "trance" created by story; rests in a musical score; *chiaroscuro*, an artist's use of dark with light; failure as "negative" learning in a science laboratory. Spiritual emptiness during a dark night of the soul becomes a time for intimate knowing: "Be still, and know…."

The soul of an institution can also undergo a dark night on the way to light. A church in Dover, Pennsylvania, literally underwent "purgation" when a fire destroyed its facility. But the pastor and lay leaders began to see this disaster as a time of spiritual purgation. At first it created a healing balm for old wounds as people rallied. But then new conflicts erupted, like saplings threatening decaying stumps. Yet today the purifying illumination draws people to a deeper union—contemplative *and* contemporary worship *and* community action.

Spiritual creativity has to do with valuing *kenosis*. As Christ "emptied himself," so Paul encourages us, "Let the same mind be in you that was in Christ Jesus" (Phil. 2:5). "Right speech comes out of silence," writes Dietrich Bonhoeffer in *Life Together*.

"Leavening the Liturgies" in this book is composed of exercises to practice being in solitude to allow the mind of Christ to baptize our agendas in community. David Tracy writes, "Moreover, Simone Weil suggests, explicitly spiritual exercises are available to anyone. Above all we can cultivate moments of tact, silence, and attentiveness to the world outside ourselves as ways of decreasing our natural egoism.... Such attention in many postmodern works on language...can also promote an attentiveness to the Void— that unavoidable reality that opens suddenly in and through our very language use."[45]

In this soul-pilgrimage toward being church for tomorrow's world, chaos is a necessary prelude to new order, what Leonard Sweet in *SoulTsunami* calls "chaordic." This process of new life out of chaos is illustrated by the diagram on the following page.

"Let the same mind be in you that was in Christ Jesus, who...emptied himself." To empty the mind is counter-cultural: "Do not be conformed to this world, but be transformed by the renewing of your minds" (Rom. 12:2). It is a paradoxical mind-set, open to surprise.

The goal of the contemplative life is not to stay in a passive void, as it might seem in some Eastern religions. *Kenosis* means living out our baptism, dying *and* rising in Christ: *surrendering* our own preconceived ideas, whether of self-inflation or self-deprecation, then *claiming* possibilities for action that have a new quality of presence. *Kenosis* is a movement from willfulness to willingness—from being conformed to the world or to other's expectations to being transformed by God's unrealized potential.

## Faith Questions "the Jesus of History": Contemporary Kenosis

Part of the loss of "soul"—the gospel's integrity, passion, and healing power— is the haunting question of whether the Jesus story is true after all, or for all. It is a topic not only in seminaries. Lay and clergy believers puzzle at what is left of the historical Jesus. Ordinary folks study Marcus Borg's *Meeting Jesus Again for the First Time;* news magazines feature the debate over what Jesus really said and did. The genie has been out of the bottle since Albert

### *Kenosis*—Emptying Preconceived Attitudes, Plans, and Ideas

"Let the same mind be in you that was in Christ Jesus, who, though he was in the form of God, did not regard equality with God as something to be exploited, but emptied himself, taking the form of a [servant], being born in human likeness. And being found in human form, he humbled himself and became obedient to the point of death—even death on a cross. Therefore God also highly exalted him..." (Phil. 2:5-9).

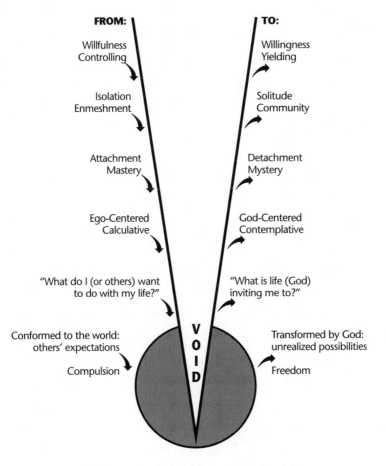

**FROM:**

Willfulness
Controlling

Isolation
Enmeshment

Attachment
Mastery

Ego-Centered
Calculative

"What do I (or others) want
to do with my life?"

Conformed to the world:
others' expectations

Compulsion

**TO:**

Willingness
Yielding

Solitude
Community

Detachment
Mystery

God-Centered
Contemplative

"What is life (God)
inviting me to?"

Transformed by God:
unrealized possibilities

Freedom

V
O
I
D

"Unless a grain of wheat falls into the earth and dies,
it remains just a single grain; but if it dies, it bears much fruit" (John 12:24).

"Do not be conformed to this world, but be transformed by the renewing
of your minds, so that you may discern what is the will of God" (Rom. 12:2).

©Kent Ira Groff and Sanford Alwine, 1992. Revised 2000. Adapted from an
anonymous source and from Kent Ira Groff *Active Spirituality: A Guide for
Seekers and Ministers* (Bethesda, Md.: The Alban Institute, 1993).

Schweitzer's classic *The Quest of the Historical Jesus* at the turn of the last century. Even somewhat conservative scholars like N. T. Wright admit Jesus' words in the Gospels reflect both second-temple Judaism and also differing voices of early Christian communities.

Yet the crisis is really an invitation to deepen spiritually, to follow the self-emptying way outlined in the *kenosis* model of Philippians 2:1-11. "Christ was in the world *incognito* and that was his *kenosis*," wrote Nicolas Berdyaev. We too must shed many of our Western privileges to identify with unbelievers.

*The real quest is to listen for the voice of Jesus through the church's tradition for the sake of the world.* The *kenosis* model is a postmodern way of understanding the classic idea of the imitation of Christ. The emptying of many traditional theological certainties can be a call to deeper trust in the truth of Christ: "You will know the truth, and the truth will make you free" (John 8:32). In *A Life of Jesus,* Japanese novelist and lay theologian Shusaku Endo presents a helpful distinction between truth and fact. The timeless truth of the Christian mystery continues to absorb the wildest scholarly conjectures.

*The truth is that God has entered the stuff of this world and is present in Christ through the Spirit to transform brokenness into blessing.* That truth is verified wherever such a transformation occurs—in the church or in the world, in nature or in human lives. It is the truth of experience, as Albert Schweitzer wrote in the concluding paragraph of *The Quest of the Historical Jesus:*

> He comes to us as One unknown, without a name, as of old, by the lake-side, He came to those...who knew him not. He speaks to us the same word: "Follow thou me!" and sets us to the tasks which He has to fulfill for our time.... And to those who obey Him, whether they be wise or simple, he will reveal Himself in the toils, the conflicts, the sufferings which they shall pass through in His fellowship, and, as an ineffable mystery, they shall learn in their own experience Who He is.[46]

The contemplative active life links the Jesus of history and the Christ of experience. As the early church contemplated the voice of Jesus beneath varied traditions, so we are called back to that same contemplative place: "My sheep hear my voice" (John 10:27). The voice of Jesus calls contemporary disciples to be contemplative activists, surrendering to the upside-down pattern of Jesus' wisdom—that the seed of faith must die in order to live.

Believing without questioning is like seed on shallow, rocky ground. Faith that questions is like seed planted in deep, dark soil: It must burst and disintegrate in order to integrate and bear fruit.

Faith questions ancient church dogma and modern Jesus research equally in order to go beyond the pages of the Bible to listen for the voice of Jesus—the very essence of Reformation theology. Mary Lathbury, a pioneering woman in ministry in the last century, understood this: "Beyond the sacred page I seek thee, Lord; / My spirit pants for thee, O Living Word." Her famous hymn, "Break Thou the Bread of Life," continues, "Bless thou the truth, dear Lord, to me, to me, / As thou didst bless the bread by Galilee." Breaking open the crust of tradition is necessary to taste the bread of true Communion. Preserving yesterday's crusty tradition will only create the stale manna of contention. (See Exod. 16:1-20; Mark 7:1-16.)

Faith questions itself, dying to old forms in order to allow new faith stories to be born in individuals, in institutions. If I am full of my own agenda and knowledge, my ears will be plugged to God's voice. To *really* pray one must be "agnostic," literally "unknowing." Only through *The Cloud of Unknowing* (to quote an anonymous medieval book title) can I shed my own attachments and listen for the voice of the Servant Lord: "Abba...for you all things are possible...yet, not what I want, but what you want" (Mark 14:36). A gospel song describes this listening well: "I Heard the Voice of Jesus Say..." To listen for the *voice* of Jesus beneath the *words* is to be contemplative active mystics. It is to embrace the upside-down wisdom of the cross: *Blessed are the poor, the gentle, the mourners, the hungry.*

And when faith questions the ultimate, the Resurrection, the invitation is to focus beyond the *facts* of what happened to the *truth* of what still happens. Vital faith enters the tomb's dark silence: emptied church tradition, bankrupt reason, or a spiritual dark night. Contemplate some emptiness in your own life. Then boldly journey outward, there to experience Christ's surprising resurrection in an ordinary gardener, a know-it-all fisher, a stranger on the road, a guest for supper!

The church has dehistoricized Jesus in sermon and art, in theology and life, making the gospel such a heavenly thing that folks cannot relate to the human Jesus. The risk and the task of active mystics in our time is to rehistoricize Jesus, as the early church did until, through contemplating the life-giving power of Christ, we burst forth as manifestations of Jesus' resurrected body in each new era.

### ALTAR WINGS

My coiled soul, my foiled self
now springs to
LIFE:
It is enough
for living resurrection faith.

But if I doubt this mystery,
wherever I see
LOVE
altaring violence
there is the risen Presence.

—Kent Ira Groff © 2000

## Repetition in the Liturgies: Reinventing the Wheel

Creative repetition is not redundancy. Corporate and personal learning are both being repeatedly woven like a shuttle—back and forth. "Back" speaks of the value of reflection on the past day, past experiences. "Forth" speaks of listening to God's invitations in the context of what lies ahead.

- **"Examen of Consciousness" (LL 38)** Reflect on your life alone (or together). Invite Christ, light of the world, to walk with you over the past day (or period of time). What are recent *gifts* in your life? (Where have you experienced being loved or loving?) *Struggles?* (Where has it been difficult to love or allow yourself to be loved?) *Invitation?* (What do you need to become more whole?) See if a word or phrase—an image or metaphor—comes to mind. Begin to repeat it, slowly, in rhythm to your breathing; or visualize it if it is an image. (Silence) Finish with a simple prayer or song like "Day by Day" or "Amazing Grace." In a group: Pair off and share with each other as comfortable (2–3 minutes each). Conclude with a few seconds of silent prayer for one another.

- **Communal Adaptation:** Invite persons to meditate on some community (committee or board) of which they are a part and to recall how they became part of this aspect of the community's life. What are the *gifts* of being in this group or community? *Struggles* in being part of it? *Invitation*—a word or phase, an image or metaphor (what you need to be more whole)? If in a group, share and conclude as above.

We see the value of "examen" in a word-symbol from Ghana. *Sankofa* depicts a bird with its feet facing forward and its head looking back, with an egg in its mouth. "Go back and fetch it" is a common translation. "The purpose of *Sankofa* is to remind us to keep an eye on the past as we continue to move ever forward."[47] Go back and fetch the essence of life: Repeated practices of reflection and engagement are the essence of dynamic liturgies for individuals, for institutions.

Yet individuals and institutions often need to recycle the same decisions. I used to complain about people "reinventing the wheel" whether they were arriving at a committee decision or working through grief or arriving at personal faith. I am less judgmental now. *I have discovered that insight is not transferable—though the desire for it is.* I recognize in myself the need to feel "ownership" in others' ideas from the bottom up before they can become my own. Like a spiral staircase, I may be at the same place, yet a different level.

The Incarnation helps me to see that patience with repetition in the finance committee can be as spiritual as repeating meaningful liturgy in worship: to go back and fetch the essence of life, to harvest "treasures of darkness" in order to reengage the world. (See Isa. 45:3.)

> ◆ **Reinventing the Wheel (LL 39)** When you find yourself repeatedly annoyed with a person or process, it may not only be you doing the wrestling. It may be God wrestling with you, angels ascending and descending, as God wrestled with Jacob. Ask, What is God trying to say *to me* through my annoyance? Or pose the question for the group, What might God be trying to say to us by noticing that we come back to this issue every six months? Allow silence before inviting responses.

Educational ministry sets the priority on formation over *in*formation. "Christ in you the hope of glory": Jesus meets us again for the first time in each new storey and story. Narrativity is the cradle for nativity, where the new life is clothed in the garb of human hospitality.

## 3. Hospitality as Education by Example

The spirituality of education has to do with communicating the welcoming God revealed in Jesus. The greatest barrier to faith is the duplicity between the church's proclamation and its lived example: "They do not practice what they teach" (Matt. 23:3). The church's showcase to the world—the *service* of worship—and its concrete acts of love are the twin touchstones where seekers learn the truth of the gospel or its nontruth. Writes Marianne Sawicki in *Seeing the Lord: Resurrection and Early Christian Practices,*

> Both of these evidences of the continuing availability of God in Jesus—the intimacy of liturgical encounter and the caring service to brothers and sisters in need—were sources of "content" for Christian teaching within those early churches which gave us the New Testament.[48]

For many a major faith barrier is a God who appears inhospitable. So one of the great tasks of education is to re-present Jesus to the world, introducing people to One who welcomes the outcast. More than that, it is to see Jesus *as* the outcast: the freaks in Flannery O'Connor's stories; "Shug" in Alice Walker's *The Color Purple*; an autistic adult in the movie *Rain Man*; a loving, innocent human being in *Forrest Gump*. Hospitality means recognizing students as our teachers, meeting seekers on their turf. To break the God barrier, short stories and films make excellent teachers. One church organized "Cinafiles," a group that sees a film and then discusses spiritual themes over pizza. *Christian* education is all about "attitude"—having "the same mind...that was in Christ Jesus, who...emptied himself."

The education of desire has to do with expecting learning to emerge from below, which is the root meaning of humility; *humus* is the low place, an unlikely source. Such moments of genuine awareness are moments when the mind is renewed while at the same time extending hospitality, even if it is to the stranger in one's own self. "Renewing of your minds" is a movement from thinking high to thinking low (Rom. 12:2).

The spirituality of education is learning to respond rather than react to the events of the world and the circumstances of one's life, in a manner that blesses the world and your own soul. Wherever this transformation happens—in a fleeting moment of worship, in a painful glimpse of self in public, in the ecstasy of a child's insight, in a self-forgetting act of altruism—we have tasted joy in sacrifice; we have experienced Eucharist.

### More Caught than Taught: Ministry of Youth with Adults

Developing reciprocal learning relationships—students and teachers with God and with one another—is the essential frame for all educational ministry, especially with youth. It is the motto of the Young Life movement: Earn the right to be heard.

Only such hospitality can give birth to Christ in the life of the believing community; only such mutuality can be the cradle for *The Godbearing Life*, to use the wonderful book title of Kenda Creasy Dean and Ron Foster. Their book's subtitle, *The Art of Soul Tending for Youth Ministry*, is a passionate plea to move from a model of ministry to youth to empowering youth to offer their spiritual gifts to the community.[49] The same is true for older adults: Unless education empowers elders' ministry for the community, it degrades the elders. Prayer practices, like many in this book, can bridge generations. Mark Yaconelli advocates a contemplative approach to youth ministry, beginning with the leadership team:

> We met for an hour before the weekly youth group to share our lives, read scripture, pray and discern our call. We understood that our desire for God would be our greatest witness to our youth, and that this meeting would keep us mindful of our own discipleship....I structured a "liturgy" that sought a balance between contemplating God and acting on behalf of youth (love of God and love of neighbor).

Yaconelli writes, "Rather than being chaperones or committee members, we wanted to be an intentional spiritual community."[50]

> ❧ **Contemplative Youth Leadership (LL 40)** Adult and youth leaders form an intentional spiritual community—engaging in spiritual practices such as the Ignatian examen of consciousness, intercessory prayer, group *lectio*, fasting, and service. The leadership becomes the model for the youth group itself. Then youth group and leaders together engage in these same spiritual practices—sometimes together, sometimes in smaller units.[51]

This kind of faith education is more caught than taught: through the example of a lived life, through experiencing the drama of suffering, rituals of joy, gestures of hospitality, attitudes of awareness. Its qualities are characterized by a movement from exterior information to interior formation—valuing space, embracing questions. And its fruit is not always some sort of measurable action in the world but rather a quality of being where one's presence becomes the action. Authentic hospitality becomes genuine education. It is the curriculum of integrity where in holy moments the giving and receiving are one. Students are my teachers. To reverse the ancient aphorism, I have discovered "when the teacher is ready, the pupil will appear."

## 4. Prayer: Awareness as Learning

"Lord, teach us to pray" is the continuing education curriculum from the morning of life through its noon and afternoon and on into its night: Yearn to learn to yearn. Such contemplative prayer begins with awareness. Notice the kinds of clothes your child is wearing; notice the lack of people of color at a public lecture; notice what set your heart aflutter during a conversation; notice the churning in your stomach at a board meeting; notice faces of people singing a hymn; and notice your feelings, whether annoyance or exuberance. Then offer the experience to God by reflecting in solitude or by sharing in community. Finally, listen for any invitation from God—a gentle nudge or a not-so-gentle shove calling you to respond. *Notice, offer, and listen.*

Luther stated the educational dimension of contemplative prayer: "Warm the heart and render praying enjoyable, filled with desire, that is the purpose":

> Frequently when I come to a certain part of Our Father or to a petition, I land in such rich thoughts that I leave behind all set prayers. When such rich, good thoughts arrive, then one should leave the other commandments aside and offer room to those thoughts and listen in stillness and for all the world not put up obstructions. For then the Holy Spirit [itself] is preaching and one word from [that] sermon is better than a thousand of our prayers. I have also often learned more from one such prayer than I would have received from much reading and writing.[52]

Learnings from prayer take a lifetime, and that is the point of Luther's words, "[One] that has prayed well has studied well." Learning to yearn moves us unawares to new levels of action. A neglected form of education is to hold retreat days right in your local church facility.

- ◦ **"Quiet Days" in Your Church (LL 41)** Using your own building for day retreats teaches that a local congregation is the primary spiritual formation center. A bare fellowship hall can be transformed with lamps, tables, plants, and rugs from persons' homes. Use the sanctuary and outdoors for periods of silent prayer—and consider installing outside benches.

# 5. Discerning as Learning

Learning means discerning. Which of the eight multiple intelligences is appropriate in a given context of learning? Anselm of Canterbury engages in several pages of contemplative prayer (*intrapersonal* intelligence) before putting forth his famous ontological argument about the existence of God (*linguistic* and *logical* intelligences). *Spatial* intelligence has to do with discerning how the room arrangement or geographical location for an interdenominational Lenten study will affect the *interpersonal* dialogue. *Kinesthetic* intelligence pays attention to movement and ritual in learning. *Musical* intelligence discerns how appropriate music can inhibit or increase awareness in a given context. *Nature* is a means to discern the patterns of life and learn from the heart of God.

> I YEARN TO LEARN
> to love as I am loved:
> Yet how exceedingly
> difficult it is to discern
> how and where,
> in what circumstances
> and by what means.
> But who?
> That is not the problem.
>
> —Kent Ira Groff © 1999

It is true that we learn from our teachers. But our teachers are often hidden in the lives of the people we are called to serve.

# CHAPTER SIX

## The Soul of Care
*"One Anothering"*

**ROMANS 12**

I appeal to you therefore, brothers and sisters, by the mercies of God, to present your bodies as a living sacrifice, holy and acceptable to God, which is your spiritual worship. Do not be conformed to this world, but be transformed by the renewing of your minds, so that you may discern what is the will of God—what is good and acceptable and perfect. **For by the grace given to me I say to everyone among you not to think of yourself more highly than you ought to think, but to think with sober judgment, each according to the measure of faith that God has assigned. For as in one body we have many members, and not all the members have the same function, so we, who are many, are one body in Christ, and individually we are members one of another.** We have gifts that differ according to the grace given to us: prophecy, in proportion to faith; **ministry, in ministering;** the teacher, in teaching; the exhorter, in exhortation; the giver, in generosity; the leader, in diligence; **the compassionate, in cheerfulness. Let love be genuine; hate what is evil, hold fast to what is good; love one another with mutual affection; outdo one another in showing honor. Do not lag in zeal, be ardent in spirit, serve the Lord. Rejoice in hope, be patient in suffering, persevere in prayer. Contribute to the needs of the saints; extend hospitality to strangers. Bless those who persecute you; bless and do not curse them. Rejoice with those who rejoice, weep with those who weep. Live in harmony with one another; do not be haughty, but associate with the lowly; do not claim to be wiser than you are. Do not repay anyone evil for evil, but take thought for what is noble in the sight of all. If it is possible, so far as it depends on you, live peaceably with all.** Beloved, never avenge yourselves, but leave room for the wrath of God; for it is written, "Vengeance is mine, I will repay, says the Lord." No, "if your enemies are hungry, feed them; if they are thirsty, give them something to drink; for by doing this you will heap burning coals on their heads." Do not be overcome by evil, but overcome evil with good.

# Let My Heart

Augustine of Hippo, 354-430
Para. Kent Ira Groff, 2000

Kent Ira Groff, 2000
Arr. Mary J. Morreale, 2000

Let my heart, such a sea of rest- less
Be the goal of my earth- ly pil- grim-

waves, find peace in you,
age, and my rest a- long

O God (O God).
the way (the way).

# The Soul of Care
## *"One Anothering"*

*Koinonía—*
## "Living in community and communion"

No guest will ever feel welcome when the host is not at home in
his own house.

> —Henri J. M. Nouwen and Walter J. Gaffney, *Aging*

"To lend each other a hand when we're falling," Brendan said.
"Perhaps that's the only work that matters in the end."

> —Frederick Buechner, *Brendan*

The man gazed at her in silence to learn whether or not the Lord
had made his journey successful.

> —Genesis 24:21

*Take a few minutes to pray. Center yourself. Ask for new ways to
"listen to Love, to love" in silence...as you read this chapter...as you
make connections with your own life and your own community of faith.*

I propose three subtle shifts from common expectations of "pastoral care" to
its more ancient name—the care of souls, or soul care. First is a shift from
pastoral care to community care, anchoring the people's well-being in ministering with one another, rather than subtle codependency on the pastor.
"Love one another as I have loved you" was spoken for all believers. "One
anothering"[55] is the meaning of *koinonía*—living in communion and community. Second is a shift from emphasizing one-to-one visitation and pastoral
counseling (often delegated to "professionals") to a broader view of soul care in

all five ministry functions—caretaking for persons *and* their environments. Third, the emphasis shifts from "doing for" to "being with": Taking care is giving the gift of presence to oneself or another—growing out of silence.

## 1. Silence and Presence: The Soul of Care

A seminary student's wife had been hospitalized for pregnancy complications, resulting in a stillbirth. She reported how lots of well-meaning students came to visit her, each trying out their latest pastoral education skills. But one student came, sat in silence, and cried with her. That, she said, was the most meaningful visit.

Silence is the prelude to being present to God, self, and others. It is "the still point of the turning world," to use a phrase from T. S. Eliot, in community or in solitude. Silence creates simplicity, shutting down the computers within and without, fasting from a multiplicity of stimuli whose demonic name is Legion if one's life is not focused and centered in God.

To still one's own soul is the bedrock of caring. "No guest will ever feel welcome when [the] host is not at home in his [or her] own house," wrote Henri J. M. Nouwen.[54] Being at home with solitude underlies any doing of value in community. Silence and its fruit of simplicity leaven the liturgies of worshiping, planning, learning, caring, and witnessing in word and deed.

### Contemplative Listening: Presence via Silence

After worship a pastor felt attacked: "Why don't you pick hymns we know?" In his "old self" he would have launched into a theological debate, but instead he found himself trying a new way. "What are some hymns that speak to you?" he asked. As the member responded, the pastor noticed a theme. He went on to ask, "I'm wondering…What's going on in your life that that these songs are so meaningful?" The person began to unburden such troubles that in a moment the barrier became a bridge.

To live out the command to love God, neighbor, and self is to begin with its first word, the Hebrew *Shema*: "Listen to Love, to love." Listen beneath the surface—to how deeply God loves you in your woundedness and your giftedness. It is the first word in Saint Benedict's *Rule*: "Listen carefully, my child, to the master's instructions, and attend to them with the ear of your heart." Only with a hearing heart can one really love another.

Contemplative listening validates others and self, empowering us for love rather than control. Active listening validates others' feelings, affirming their concern before responding. Contemplative listening slows down the rapid pace by adding the dimension of pausing to ponder the question: What might God be saying *to me* through this brother or sister? Contemplative listening means converting my insight into a question—What would it be like if...?—or telling a story that persists in my consciousness. It can mean being directive: to invite persons to pause, to listen to the echo of their words. The best response may be no answer but merely the gift of the other's feeling heard; or it may be receiving an insight myself, conveying spiritual self-esteem for the other. Contemplative listening is helpful in personal encounters—in our family rooms, lunchrooms, workrooms, and boardrooms.

Interviewing with a pastor search committee, a candidate noticed that while several asked questions about programs and finances, one younger man had been asking about prayer and the spiritual life. Later the pastor asked him what experiences prompted his interest in prayer and the spiritual life of the community. The story he heard was that this man's wife had recently died and he was single-parenting his son—a situation similar to the pastor's experience as the primary caregiver for his preschool son. Each had "listened beneath" the other's words, which is the true meaning of *ob-audio*, the Latin root for "obedience." The care of souls had already emerged in the search process itself before the official call to ministry.

## Ministry of Creative Absence: Silence as Presence

The art of soul care is to know the time for a ministry of creative presence and for a ministry of creative absence. An attitude of "fasting" from a compulsive need to minister can free us from always running to give help or advice and can actually empower another.

Jesus delayed two days before going to see Lazarus. Can we trust a radical ministry of absence—sometimes by choice, sometimes by circumstance—to be a sign of great love? (See John 11:5, 36.) It may be as valuable as a visit to spend half an hour in prayer for another; to listen to a recording of the person's favorite music as intercession; to call the person or a family member, offering to pray on the phone; to donate blood on the person's behalf; to babysit his or her children or cook a meal. Other times, precisely the way to help is *not to help*: to break a situation of codependence, to make it necessary for another to draw on his or her own resources, to find new friends, to take initiative.

This ministry of absence is reflected in the way we say good-bye. "The words of Jesus, 'It is for your good that I leave' should be part of every pastoral call we make," Henri J. M. Nouwen wrote in *The Living Reminder*.[55] The Lord's Table celebrates the presence but also the absence of the risen One, "until Christ comes again." In *The Gulag Archipelago* Alexander Solzhenitsyn speaks of the value of how people leave each other: that one never knows if it may be the last time before one is imprisoned or killed or disappeared. My friend Sasha Makovkin describes this Russian tradition. Before anyone leaves another's home, the oldest woman calls everyone present to sit with the departing visitor in silence, then one by one to stand and embrace the person with a blessing.

Good-byes are formative in soul care. A woman tells how the most meaningful part of worship is the benediction: two arms upraised in silence, as if embracing everyone with love, just before the spoken blessing. For another it is a simple signing of the cross. In contrast, the single raised hand meant to bless can actually appear to push folks away or even conjure images for some of a Nazi salute. Contemplate your gestures and how they are seen in local context and tradition and new ones that can bless others.

> **Passing the Peace (LL 42)** Cue people with a greeting like, "The peace of Christ be with you!" (instead of, "Hey, Joe, how was your golf game?"). This kinesthetic blessing can be given to several lonely neighbors in the pews in just a few minutes. Suggest gazing into another's eyes as a prayer for God's best—even to some you cannot physically greet. As a worship leader, use this "prayer with a glance" to visually welcome back persons who have been ill or away.

Omitting the peace and letting people greet haphazardly at the end of worship usually means friends greet only friends, while others make a bee-line to see someone about a "task." A quick exit, a dismissive tilt of the head can negate our best intentions. How we leave one another is how we will be implanted in others' spiritual memory.

Healthy *koinonía* offers life-giving rituals to bless persons leaving their churches, their jobs, their relationships or being commissioned to a mission experience away from home. In her insightful book, *Praying Our Goodbyes*, Joyce Rupp spells out stages of our leavings and grievings: *recognition, reflection, ritualization*—all necessary steps toward *reorientation*.[56]

A young adult tells how after only a one-year sojourn with a Mennonite church (which he never joined), on his last Sunday the congregation called him forward for the laying on of hands and sent him forth with their prayers. As in the book of Acts, this act was a lasting benediction of the community, not just of a pastor.

What does it mean to be an apostolic community? Before leaving on my sabbatical to India, I received such a blessing from my parachurch community at Oasis Ministries. We need to make such a sending forth of others a normal part of our worshiping communities. (See LL 53, "Rituals of Sending.")

### THE ART OF SOUL CARE

Listening—that essential bedrock of grace
incarnate in this its first flesh,
communing spirit to spirit, unconditionally;

Loving—a caring spiritual presence with another
through dark valley, with rod and staff
comforting while gently confronting;

Learning—mutually with others, self, God,
linking the mind's corporate taproot
with tradition and creativity in community;

Laughing—that good medicine of a merry heart,
in belief, in disbelief, like Sarah and Abraham—
the humor of light moments, mistakes, mystery;

Leaving—praying our goodbyes, equipping saints
for their own inter- and intra-dependence,
from external counselors to internal Counselor.

To listen to love to learn to laugh to leave,
is a movement of the Spirit revealing
the Mystery hidden for ages in each and all—
    wounded healers healing,
    beggars showing other beggars
    where to find bread.

             —Kent Ira Groff © 1990

Silence is the bedrock of presence. We see it in the encounter of Abraham's servant, sent to find Rebekah as a wife for Isaac: "The man gazed at her in silence to learn whether or not the Lord had made his journey successful" (Gen. 24:21). In Egypt as Joseph finally discloses himself to his abusive siblings, "his brothers could not answer him, so dismayed were they at his presence" (Gen. 45:3). Silence can create space for expressing speechless love.

## The Churches' Silence on Abuse—and the Gift of Sexuality

Silence, however, can be painful for persons silenced through violence or oppression. The care of souls means tuning our ear to stifled voices of abused women and children, of men or women in dead-end careers—caught between eking out their survival and selling their soul to dehumanizing systems. We must not act naively, as if silence is always "golden."

*One reason many of us resist solitude is because our painful memories of being silenced by family and society reemerge.* It is important to acknowledge this truth from time to time—in worship, in groups, in print. Yet our pain is all the more reason not to avoid but to incorporate safe places and silent spaces for healing soul care in worship, small groups, and one-to-one spiritual friendship.

Just as churches are silent about the abuse of sex, they are silent about the gift of sexuality. I define sexuality as our divinely given desire for loving, life-giving intimacy that nurtures all areas of life—which often gets distorted as only the physical act of sex. If tomorrow's church is to recover the passion and compassion of Jesus, we must break its stained-glass silence about the gift of sexuality. The Word became flesh, and the intensity of sexual passion embodies our deepest spiritual hungers, woundings, and bliss. Sexual longings beckon to divine Joy, and even tragic sexual woundings can mysteriously become the occasion to seek God as Lover.

Today's sex-saturated culture creates a golden opportunity to break the silence and point directly to spiritual dimensions of sexuality in all of life through film and story, song and poetry. A lay minister conducts a "spiritual life assessment" by asking, What is your favorite love song? Answers often reveal clues about a person's image of God. Inspired by the biblical Song of Solomon, mystics like John of the Cross used sexual language to describe spiritual woundings and joy: "All things ceased. I went out from myself."

And in acts of genuine altruism when one goes outside oneself, positive endorphins are released as in orgasm, which in French is *le petit mort*, "the little death." The Bible speaks of sexual-spiritual generativity, which occurs as little deaths in this life are transformed into expressions of justice and love; "bearing fruit" does not just mean having babies. Tillie Olsen writes in *Silences* of women and some men whose voices had been silenced for years—but later redeemed, as fertile gifts of writing or art had been gestating.

As sexual attitudes change, we need to speak openly of sexuality as a *terrific* thing—exhilarating yet frightening, to be celebrated *and* protected according to each one's vocation. Worship is all about validating people's experiences of joy *and* pain in the presence of God. We can care for isolated souls in con-

versations, classrooms, and sanctuaries—not always needing an entire sermon. Simply to acknowledge the rejection of minorities, silenced women or
voiceless children, gay persons or childless couples, creates a movement from
negative silence to healing silence.

The Daytime Emmy Awards honored Fred Rogers of TV's *Mister Rogers'
Neighborhood* for lifetime achievement. His acceptance speech followed a dreary
sequence of put-downs and off-color jokes. In contrast, Rogers asked his audience to take ten seconds to think of "people who helped you become who you
are today." As this roomful of TV stars and producers sat in silence, some of
them had tears streaming down their faces. Imagine it: *just ten seconds* could
bring to the surface such hidden hunger.

People are starving for mentors who connect their inner lives with their
outer worlds. Anyone reading these pages can do what Fred Rogers did. Lay
disciples can be the catalysts for that hidden wholeness, as Thomas Merton
named it, to come to the surface in the confrontations and celebrations in
work places and home spaces where most clergy cannot enter.

## 2. Hospitality: Soul Care in the Service

I was sitting with hundreds of people at a memorial service for a friend who
given himself to alleviate world hunger, yet who had caved in to despair,
taking his own life. Meditating during the prelude music, I was overcome
with silent grieving, then sobbing. Drying my tears, I felt a hand on my
shoulder, and turned around to meet a sisterly gaze. Kinesthetic, spatial,
musical, intrapersonal, and interpersonal hospitality converged in a powerful moment of soul care in worship.

Part of the art of the beauty is in the weaving. Silence is so interlaced with
pastoral care because quietly *being with* hurting people (contemplation) is the
foundation for any meaningful *doing for* others (manifestation). In this tapestry the place where community care ends and outreach or education or worship begin cannot be so clear cut.

Though reared in a church family, Todd had gone through a decade of rebel-
lion and loneliness, addiction and atheism, and now found himself in Minneapolis in his mid-twenties. He had decided to move to Washington, D.C.,
hoping for more friends, better luck. But on his last weekend, he felt bad
about never having gone to church with his roommate, Will, so he offered to
go this final Sunday. What happened was overwhelming. Twenty to thirty

people, all strangers, came up to greet him: Are you Will's friend? Then you're our friend too. We love having you here. We want to be your church. Good luck in Washington. If you ever come back to Minneapolis, come see us....The genuine hospitality of it all rang in his ears for days: *He felt loved by God.* Canceling his proposed move, he stayed a year and joined that church—and somewhere along the way he felt drawn to ordained ministry. Today Todd is a pastor, and the theology that guides him is that people have to experience human love before they can believe in divine love—and that the way it happens is often serendipitous.

A brief line in a sermon or a worship cue can raise consciousness of hospitality and validate the marginalized: Mention the courage it takes for a newly single person to return to church; for a visitor to enter a church after years away from church; for a freshly grieving spouse to decide to sit in different pew, only to receive an angry glare from a long-term pew-sitter; for youth to offer their musical and cultural gifts that shock adults; for victims of male abuse to get beyond "Our Father" in our hymns and prayers.

In *Seeing the Lord: Resurrection and Early Christian Practices*, Marianne Sawicki, writes of this integration of soul care and service:

> In contemporary pastoral theology, consensus is forming that the criterion of effective teaching or preaching is its ability to coordinate, interpret, and sustain both the church's life of worship and its life of service to the world...intrinsically linked to both its celebration and its actualization of God's kingdom.[57]

Jan Hus Presbyterian Church in New York City, like many city churches, found its congregation dwindling, while at the same time the church was hosting a variety of groups during the week who appreciated the use of the building. Yet there seemed to be no link between the weekday groups and the Sunday worshipers. The sanctuary was locked during the week, and the church's session had a representative stationed in the hallways to protect the church in case of difficulties. Then someone discovered a connection: What if the church representative's job description were to shift from protection to hospitality? Tables were set up with a welcoming host and literature about the church's worship and programs; the sanctuary was unlocked during the times of the community meetings with an invitation to enter and pray. Soon people from the weekday groups began to participate in the life of the church—and a revitalized congregation is the result today.

Too much one-to-one pastoral care can actually create dysfunctional relationships and play into a culture of codependence. Some people when they come together become more than they are separately—healthy community. But others, when they come together, become less than they are—dysfunctional community. Couple relationships can be either healthy or dysfunctional too. *Why?* I have pondered.

A hint has begun to occur to me. Healing occurs in going outside my own expertise and environment into someone else's and in processing the experiences. Volunteer projects can be life-giving, as I have discovered many times over for my own soul's sake.

I have just returned from working on a house for Habitat for Humanity in Harrisburg, Pennsylvania. One part of me had wanted to spend the day writing this book, but another part knew that engaging in this kind of kinesthetic service might actually be soul care for myself. The volunteer housing project won out—and amazingly I discovered I was still writing on soul care as I reflected while working. For as volunteer builders come and go, each leaving their less-than-perfect door jambs and window sills, a radical kind of therapy is created. Anyone expecting the perfect house will walk off the job by 9 A.M.! It is worth several visits to a psychiatrist to rediscover that constructing genuine community means building on one another's less-than-perfect beginnings.

A trip to Haiti redirected a physician's life. Helping adjudicated youth write poetry ignites the spirit of a disillusioned attorney. Inviting such disciples to share a Worship Interview multiplies the pastoral care. (See LL 13.)

## 3. Prayer: The Laboratory of Soul Care

Prayer is to religion as the laboratory is to science: the place of experimentation, testing, and learning—positive or negative. *One reason churches soft-pedal spiritual practices is our underlying doubt and fear concerning the validity of prayer.*

Everyone has sensed in a crowd when someone was watching. Invite a youth or confirmation class to try the following experiment, then ask the members to report in a "Worship Interview," thereby leavening the community's understanding and analogies to prayer.

    Youth Awareness Lab (LL 43) Ask the youth to focus energies on one who volunteers to be blindfolded and who then sits in the center of a circle. In a few minutes, give a signal to release the focus. The blindfolded person usually feels the shift. Ask: If we can experience normal human energies across a room, why not in Germany? or Ghana?

The "Awareness Lab" is a simple experiment, yet no less profound than noticing my heart rate increase after twenty minutes of walking this morning. Intercessory prayer taps human energies and focuses them Godward with love toward others. Larry Dossey, M.D., in books like *Recovering the Soul: A Scientific and Spiritual Search* and *Prayer Is Good Medicine,* shows a scientific correlation between prayer and health.[58] Churches are called to be laboratories of prayer. To paraphrase Søren Kierkegaard, if I assume that prayer changes the pray-er, I am never disappointed. "History belongs to the intercessors, who believe a new world into being," writes Walter Wink in *Engaging the Powers.*[59] Prayer is the essential thread in the web of work for justice: It saves the workers and the world from triumphalism.

### Restoring the Soul of Prayer to Care

There is a host of ways to extend the soul of prayer through ordinary disciples' ministries: corporate worship, small groups or "class meetings" as in Wesleyan tradition, lay programs such as Stephen Ministries or a parish nurse, spiritual companionship or formal spiritual direction with trained lay or clergy guides, a "prayer-care line" phone device with a devotional message, creative newsletters, outreach projects that nurture one's soul while serving others, and leavening structures and committees with time for faith sharing.

Yet worship proclaims by ethos and example more than by sermons whether a community lives up to what is printed on many church bulletins: "Ministers—All Members of the Church." The so-called "pastoral prayer" is a telltale clue.

### The Pastoral Prayer—or Prayers of the People?

"As far as I am concerned, the 'pastoral prayer' is one of the major problems in Protestant worship," writes William Willimon in *Worship as Pastoral Care.*[60] How strange that the Reformation made "the priesthood of all believers" a cornerstone of renewal, yet today in many Protestant churches the pastor offers the pastoral prayer as a monologue on behalf of the people and the world and is responsible that no name or cause is missed.

Thrusting a pastor into the role of solo priest denies the believers' priesthood. Protestant pastors are still expected to be the primary or sole representative to visit the hospital and personally to take Communion to homebound members, a secret reason for infrequent Communion. "We wouldn't want to burden you (and ourselves) every week!" Thanks to increased use of intinction and a common cup, such "reasons" are lessening.

In contrast, when I visit many Catholic and Episcopal or Pentecostal and evangelical churches, large or small, I find it refreshing to be given permission to speak forth (or whisper) my concerns during "the prayers of the people." Even to gather written concerns to be included by the pastor and allow for spontaneous whispered prayer offerings is a gift of participation. (See LL 44 below.) In fact, many so-called "liturgical" churches have trained cadres of lay folks as "eucharistic ministers" to visit and take Communion to homebound members. "You are...a royal priesthood...God's own people" (1 Pet. 2:9).

What has gone wrong? Like many other aspects of the Reformation, some things have reversed themselves. I have visited churches where concerns that were on everyone's mind are unnamed—like the Sunday after Rodney King was beaten in Los Angeles or the Sunday after the bombings began in Iraq and Kosovo—and for a worshiper to name such concerns aloud would feel out of place or appear as a put-down to the pastor.

Yet that is our purpose as priests—to name and bear the community's concerns before God. "Bear one another's burdens" (Gal. 6:2) was never written to clergy only! It is part of our "one anothering." In churches that invite people to lift their concerns before God, headlined world issues and local needs invariably make it into the prayers.

~ **Participatory Prayers (LL 44)** Worship leaders: Avoid a monologue and create optional ways to be priests to one another. Use seasons of the church year to experiment with varied methods like the following:

1. Keep each section of prayers to a minute or so in length, with a sung or spoken congregational response* between each section: thanksgivings, intercessions for the church and world, supplication for ourselves.

2. Do not try the following alone. Enlist choir, staff, and board member support to lead by example; then invite people: (a.) to *speak forth* their joys clearly during thanksgivings and their concerns during intercessions (repeat if necessary through a microphone); or for large churches: (b.) to *whisper* the names and concerns during the intercessions, creating spiritual and

psychological participation; or (c.) to *print* their requests and names on small cards, which will be brought forward for the leader to name during the prayers; or (d.) to *come forward* and actually *lead the prayers themselves*: Train persons to say only a sentence or two. As worship leader, hold the mike for each person; then offer a summary prayer for causes that may have been missed.

3. Highlight names (persons with prayer concerns) printed in the worship bulletin; an usher then asks some worshiper(s) on arriving to be in silent prayer for the highlighted name(s) during the service and in the week ahead. (Or names on cards can be read aloud, then given to members to pray for in the week ahead.)

4. Try other participatory methods: Practice "pause and pray" yourself throughout the service, and invite worshipers to do so. Try "Prayer Teams during Worship" (LL 46); create sentences for "Balancing the Lord's Prayer" (LL 18) with feminine images.

*Sing or say responses before, during, and after prayers. Try a simple Taizé chant (varied with church seasons): "Wait for the Lord" or "Kyrie" or "O Lord, Hear Our Prayer"[61] or a line of a hymn or a spiritual such as "Someone's Praying, Lord" (from "Kum Ba Yah") or a chant from this book.

## *Outpatient Treatment: Models for Community Soul Care*

I recall Bea sitting at our dinner table in the '80s, telling how her husband Ray would have cataract surgery the next week. Ray quickly chimed in that it would be outpatient surgery, so that I (his pastor) would not visit him—yet he expressed normal fears about the "simple" procedure. Later in the conversation, speaking of another member's hand surgery, Bea said, "Didn't you visit her in the hospital? Oh, that's right, hers was outpatient too!"

This seed of experience was implanted in my mind. Fears for the outpatient are just as real as for the inpatient. Prolonged radiation or chemotherapy, psychotherapy or infertility sessions are often grueling for patient and family. But it is unrealistic for a minister to head off to bless each person's concern in a therapist or doctor's office or outpatient clinic. The conflict of this medical reality provides a rationale for restoring biblically based community soul care. (See James 5:13-16.)

↪ **A Service of Wholeness (LL 45)** At least monthly offer an opportunity to pray and receive prayers in a service of wholeness (and/or in regular worship, below) for spiritual, emotional, physical, vocational, family, or institutional pain. Offer anointing with oil as a sign of blessing all means of healing—noting the rationale above.

↪ **Prayer Teams during Worship (LL 46)** Train lay teams to offer personalized prayers as part of worship. (Ask the person's concern; offer a brief prayer.) Any may request prayers for themselves or others, coming to teams of two stationed in corners of the sanctuary during the singing of hymns, returning to the pew after communing—or after worship in an adjacent room.

↪ **Alternate Worship Times—and Communion (LL 47)** Offer alternate worship times besides Sunday morning. If you do not offer Communion weekly, offer it in a chapel-like area or parlor after each service for those who desire. Consider a brief Saturday or Sunday afternoon Eucharist when homebound persons can be transported by young adults or family to revisit their own house of worship with its memories, smells, and sights.

↪ **Contemplative Prayer Group (LL 48)** Create or revitalize a prayer group with contemplative practices—Taizé chants, African American spirituals, praise choruses, centering prayer, or scripture sharing (Resource II). Mention personal, local, and world concerns for violence, disasters, human rights. Then pray in silence for several minutes. Then members may share how they were drawn to pray. *Such groups are a safe place to experiment with complementary worship— both contemplative and contemporary forms.*

↪ **Convert a Broom Closet (LL 49)** Most church sanctuaries are locked, unheated in winter and hot in summer, so people no longer stop by to pray. Yet they go to the church office to submit a newsletter article. Why not both? Every church ought to have a small accessible prayer chapel or meditation room—a Mennonite congregation calls theirs the "sabbath room"—where Cheyenne on her way to work or Tyrone on his way home can stop off for prayer.

Soul care grounded in God frees us from defensiveness. Freda A. Gardner, recent Moderator of the Presbyterian Church (USA), said, "God will protect the church and take care of God's self. Our job is to take care of each other." It is the essence of *koinonía*: "Love one another with mutual affection; outdo one another in showing honor....Rejoice with those who rejoice, weep with those who weep" (Rom. 12:10, 15).

Another key for the care of souls is extending hospitality to prospective disciples. In chapter 7 we explore community building with visitors outside the membership circle.

IN
YOUR
CARE
Know this well:
when souls are in your care, I will bear them safely, gracefully into
a place, a sacred space not in your ability or responsibility
to name
or claim.

—Kent Ira Groff © 1997

## 4. Discerning Love: Empower One Another

Here are some ground rules for discernment in all five ministry functions. First, develop a "covenant of ethical guidelines" to be signed by all professional and volunteer ministers. Let these guidelines not merely be prohibitive rules against abusive behavior but also include preventive practices agreed on by the community, "a covenant for healthy soul care." (See Resource VIII.) Sexual or spiritual abuse by leaders leaves indelible wounds on the souls of seekers and long-term disciples. A bright, committed lay disciple fell into destructive sexual relationships. He knew what happened: "I burned myself out and I set myself up." Sexuality is integrally related to our deepest spiritual longings, sufferings, and joys. It is a terrific gift, to be honored and guarded.

Second, develop internal guidelines to discern when it is best that ordained pastors be present in times of crisis and celebration, with or without lay ministers. But make them guidelines, not rules. Redundant pastoral care can be healthy or unhealthy: Is it complementary or competitive? After a dozen lay ministers and a pastor had showed up to visit a patient, a critical care nurse asked, "How many ministers does your church have?!" Competitive care may occur in areas like worship leadership or teaching. It is often caused by ministers who fall into two traps: *pleasers* who have not learned creative ways of being present through absence and *manipulators* whose control needs cannot let go and empower others. In both cases, the spiritual need is detachment. Finding a physical gesture to express relinquishment on a daily basis can help.

Third, develop or take advantage of contemplative training in basic pastoral and spiritual skills: visiting hospitals, prisons, and homes; welcoming and integrating new members; serving as prayer teams in worship; providing spiritual direction for seekers and members; developing outreach ministries. Such training provides ways for leaders and members to discern their gifts and respond to their call.

The contemplative thread of discernment can be woven into church life in the form of the Quaker model of a "clearness committee." Members can offer this process of soul care to any who want to discern their sense of calling at any stage of life. (See Kevin's experience in chapter 7 below.)

- **The Clearness Committee (LL 50)** Originally developed by the Friends for discernment for marriage, the Clearness Committee is adapted now for individuals facing a variety of vocational struggles. The "focus" person seeking clearness consults with a prayerful colleague and chooses participants from various contexts of life. The focus person then writes up his or her situation in advance and circulates it to these five or six trusted persons, choosing one who is prayerful to serve as convener, another as note taker. The meeting begins with silence and prayer, then a fresh statement of the concern by the focus person. This is followed by silence, then by discerning questions ("Have you considered...?") or observations ("I'm hearing four possible careers..."), but not "fix-it" advice ("Why don't you...?"). All discussion takes place in a prayerful atmosphere and may end with the laying on of hands in prayer. The group may be reconvened.[62] Option: A personal life mission statement or a powerful dream or spiritual experience could be included as data for reflection with a Clearness Committee.

- **Corporate Clearness Committee (LL 51)** The above model can also be convened for clergy, staff, and lay leadership to gain a sense of clarity for the community's vision and ministries.

## 5. Faith Stories as Corporate Soul Care

In *Transforming Church Boards into Communities of Spiritual Leaders,* Charles Olsen recounts how at a board retreat of Westminster Church, elders were invited to identify a meaningful congregational story. They chose the baptism of Mikey, a twelve-year-old boy with a mental disability whose foster family was joining Westminster. At a meeting authorizing the baptism of two of the family's biological children, one elder had casually asked, "But what about Mikey?" After discussing the meaning of baptism and with the guidance of the Presbyterian *Book of Order*, elders decided to interview Mikey, the foster family, and Mikey's biological mother. All the "parents" agreed that Mikey held a simple love and trust in Jesus and supported his baptism and faith journey.

> On the appointed day for his baptism, the congregation was caught off guard when Mikey burst into a loud, joyful laugh as the water ran off his head. Then they were deeply moved to see his smile as he beamed his way up the aisle during his presentation and introduction to the congregation![63]

### Paradigm Stories: Spiritual Direction for Community

Mikey's story became a parable and paradigm for Westminster church. Members began to define opportunities for ministries with alternately abled children and their families, relating their story to the biblical story of Philip baptizing the marginalized Ethiopian eunuch (Acts 8:26-39). When the human story intersects the divine story, ministry happens. Yet the story began with deep, soul-searching questions about baptizing Mikey.

Like the parables of Jesus our stories are bracketed by questionings, and one anothering means staying with what is unresolved—even finding a gift in it. When I feel like "a flimsy web of questions" myself, to use Denise Levertov's phrase,[64] I am more able to be hospitable to others' unrest—which miraculously gets woven into my story.

### Good Medicines: Stories as Soul Care

A great burden of soul care is discouragement, and a spiritual prescription is to practice the art of recollection: to recall regenerative experiences, renewing moments of God's presence (see Ps. 77:11-12). Abraham Heschel said that much of the Bible could be summarized in one word: *Remember*. One's solitary story can become a paradigm for the community, as with Moses' encounter with the burning bush (Exod. 3:1-16).

The faith dimension may not immediately be visible in one's normal work-a-day world. Soul care happens when seekers find a safe place to recount their ordinary experiences in community and, in the process, to sense the Presence *incognito*. "Surely the Lord is in this place—and I did not know it" (Gen. 28:16).

In *Sharing the Journey: Support Groups and America's New Quest for Community,* Robert Wuthnow confirms how shared stories of grief and glimpses of hope create life-giving healing.

A congregation had experienced a score of deaths in one year. Morale was at a low ebb. One night the pastor was driving home, wearied from yet another "grief call," when the thought struck that these folks could minister to one another. Within a short time a grief support group had been formed, and it remains a major outreach ministry of that congregation twenty years later. The formation of the grief ministry created a "paradigm shift" for a discouraged faith community who from that point took on other incredible forms of new life.

In the early 1970s I presented a paper for an area meeting of the Society of Biblical Literature at Duquesne University in Pittsburgh. In late afternoon the presider introduced me, the last presenter: "And now the paper we have all been waiting for, 'Bultmann, Pannenberg, and Kunta Kinte.'" (I would connect Kunta's suffering in the hold of the slave ship with Jesus' crucifixion.) Such fear gripped me that I trembled. Knowing nothing in those days of breath prayers, I never recovered, even during questions and answers. I was so shamed that I never again presented to such a group, though now I lecture at seminaries.

Twenty years later, I experienced a powerful healing of perception. Nancy Bieber, a staff member of Oasis Ministries, was speaking to a group: "We are called the Society of Friends, but also Quakers—which comes from the fact that a Friend rising to speak may 'quake,' a sign of speaking a truth greater than oneself." In a moment of community, a simple comment transmitted spiritual healing for this haunting inner wound of two decades.

Church happens whenever we gather to rehearse our death-in-life stories and see ourselves in the life-in-death Story that transforms brokenness into blessing—for one's own soul and for the cosmos. The world is filled with Eucharist. In *Women Who Run with the Wolves,* Clarissa Pinkola Estés writes,

> I hope you will go out and let stories happen to you, and that you will work them, water them with your blood and tears and your laughter till they bloom, till you yourself burst into bloom. Then you will see what medicines they make, and where and when to apply them. That is the work. The only work.[65]

It is impossible not to be in ministry if you live in genuine community and in communion with God.

# CHAPTER SEVEN

# The Soul of Outreach
## *Mutual Hospitality*

**ROMANS 12**

I appeal to you therefore, brothers and sisters, by the mercies of God, to present your bodies as a living sacrifice, holy and acceptable to God, which is your spiritual worship. Do not be conformed to this world, but be transformed by the renewing of your minds, so that you may discern what is the will of God—what is good and acceptable and perfect. **For by the grace given to me I say to everyone among you not to think of yourself more highly than you ought to think, but to think with sober judgment, each according to the measure of faith that God has assigned.** For as in one body we have many members, and not all the members have the same function, so we, who are many, are one body in Christ, and individually we are members one of another. We have gifts that differ according to the grace given to us: prophecy, in proportion to faith; ministry, in ministering; the teacher, in teaching; the exhorter, in exhortation; **the giver, in generosity; the leader, in diligence; the compassionate, in cheerfulness. Let love be genuine; hate what is evil, hold fast to what is good;** love one another with mutual affection; outdo one another in showing honor. **Do not lag in zeal, be ardent in spirit, serve the Lord. Rejoice in hope, be patient in suffering, persevere in prayer. Contribute to the needs of the saints; extend hospitality to strangers. Bless those who persecute you; bless and do not curse them. Rejoice with those who rejoice, weep with those who weep. Live in harmony with one another; do not be haughty, but associate with the lowly; do not claim to be wiser than you are. Do not repay anyone evil for evil, but take thought for what is noble in the sight of all. If it is possible, so far as it depends on you, live peaceably with all. Beloved, never avenge yourselves, but leave room for the wrath of God; for it is written, "Vengeance is mine, I will repay, says the Lord." No, "if your enemies are hungry, feed them; if they are thirsty, give them something to drink; for by doing this you will heap burning coals on their heads." Do not be overcome by evil, but overcome evil with good.**

# Christ Is the Icon of God Unseen

Tune: Land of Rest CM

Kent Ira Groff, 1991

American folk melody
Harm. Annabel Morris Buchanan, 1938
Adapt. Mary J. Morreale, 2000

1. Christ is the i-con of God un-seen, cre-a-tion's source and goal, through whom all things are still cre-a-ted, our des-ti-ny su-preme.
2. Christ is the head o-ver church and cos-mos, the source of life re-born, God's love em-bod-ied, heal-ing wounds, peace mak-ing through the cross.
3. In times when we are es-tranged and hos-tile, through e-vil powers or deeds, God's un-de-feat-ed love will tri-umph, for-give and re-con-cile.
4. Bap-tized, now bur-ied with Christ and raised, lift up your hearts and minds! Put on the cloth-ing of com-pas-sion. In word and deed give praise!

# The Soul of Outreach
## Mutual Hospitality

*Apostolé*—
"Being sent and sending forth"

Feed my sheep....I have other sheep....Just as you did it to even
one of the least of these, my brothers and sisters, you did it to me.

—**Jesus in John 21:17; 10:16; Matt. 25:40 (AT)**

In the reception of the poor and of pilgrims the greatest care and
solicitude should be shown, because it is especially in them that
Christ is received.

—*The Rule of St. Benedict*

Our being Christians today will be limited to two things: prayer
and righteous action among [people]. All Christian thinking,
speaking, and organizing must be born anew out of this prayer
and action.

—Dietrich Bonhoeffer, *Letters and Papers from Prison*

Though it finds no name for [the Divine], whenever the afflicted
are loved for themselves alone, it is God who is present. God is not
present even if we invoke [God], where the afflicted are merely
regarded as an occasion for doing good.

—Simone Weil, *Waiting for God*

*Take a few minutes to pray. Center yourself. As you read, ask, What
would it mean to practice hospitality in all areas of my life? in worshiping, organizing, learning, caring for others, witnessing in word
and deed? in personal, family, and corporate life?*

Hospitality is embodied spirituality. The word *spirituality* by itself sounds disembodied, yet it is presently culture's term of choice: "I've developed my spirituality, but I'm not religious"—meaning not interested in institutional religion. Sometimes a person making this statement is on a quest for privatized spirituality. Yet many seekers genuinely do want to develop an embodied spirituality with compassion and social concern but have found institutional churches lacking that very connection.

One way to convey that life in God is grounded in the life of the world is to avoid using the word *spirituality* alone: Speak of the spiritual life, spiritual formation, spiritual practices, or spiritual community. Otherwise, like yesterday's musty *piety*, given two or more generations *spirituality* will be mothballed as irrelevant, even dangerous. Fixating on personal religious experience without connecting with the suffering life of this fragile planet is diabolic: "Get behind me Satan!" (Matt. 16:23). It is to deny the Christ who became flesh. That is the root meaning of the word *diabolic: dividing*, a body at war with itself.

This chapter is all about embodied spirituality: connecting one's life in God in a way that blesses the world. Hospitality embodies the integrity, passion, and wholeness of Christ. Yet organizational religion often suffocates the life-giving organism, leaving wineskins without wine.

Earlier I offered a definition of spiritual formation: "Learning to respond rather than react to the events of the world and the circumstances of one's life in a manner that blesses the world and your own soul." The new wine of spiritual experience needs the messy membrane of community to embody it in the world of action.

## 1. Hospitality as Reciprocity and Simplicity

Hospitality grounds spiritual experience in the stuff of this world: "The Word became flesh and tented among us" (John 1:14, AT). Hospitality is the soul of mission, at home while always on the move. Its paradigm and paradox is Christ on the way with us to Emmaus: The journey is home; stranger becomes friend; guest becomes host—the divine in human guise, epiphany in breaking ordinary bread. (See Luke 24:13-35.)

Hospitality is Abraham and Sarah, entertaining three strangers and receiving the laughable promise of birth in old age; Joseph, sold into slavery by his siblings, later feeding his estranged family in Egypt; the prophet Elijah and the widow of Zarephath sustained by a flask of oil and a jar of meal. It is Mary

giving birth amid animals in an overcrowded guesthouse; a Samaritan helping a wounded journeyer; a fisher on the shore inviting, "Come and have
breakfast" (John 21:12). Hospitality is Jesus' acid test of genuine spiritual
experience: "Just as you did it to even one of the least of these, my brothers
and sisters, you did it to me" (Matt. 25:40, AT). Hospitality protects outreach
from paternalism: It speaks of reciprocity, paradoxically receiving in the very
act of giving—an intersection of the divine in a human encounter.

"To live together in a world with porous borders" is the challenge of the
millennium, according to Justice Sandra Day O'Connor, speaking at Chau-
tauqua, New York, on August 13, 1999. If something goes wrong in Japan's
market it can affect jobs in the U.S. Yet we have trouble transferring this
global business sense practically in local faith communities.

An individual or congregation living as if cut off from the global community denies the body of Christ—like shutting down our breathing appa-
ratus, severing brain from body (Col. 1:15-22). And like breathing, genuine
community is marked by simplicity and complexity, because just to breathe
in solitude is to participate in the oneness of the cosmos. Like inspiration and
expiration, the life-giving organism of the faith community needs the creative rhythm of receiving and giving. It may not always look like outreach.
The Dead Sea is not dead: Its outlet is the sky, creating organic deposits.

Hospitality goes beyond a mere balancing. It is a recognition that in the
resurrection life of the Spirit we may, in rare moments, experience the union
of prayer and action, giving and receiving, divine presence in human guise—
a foretaste of heaven on earth.

An American pastor on sabbatical in Nigeria experienced hospitality after
being robbed. In a country where inflation and poverty are merciless, he wrote,

> You can imagine how we felt when the entire church leadership
> showed up on our doorstep a week later to bring their sympathy for
> being robbed and to present us with a special collection they had
> raised for us! We were speechless. Such generosity is hard to
> comprehend. They felt so bad that I had experienced violence while
> a guest in their country. We have so much in comparison, of course,
> and there was part of me that was embarrassed that they were giving
> us so much out of their poverty. Yet there was no question that the
> gift had to be received. We will find other ways to share it with
> others but had to honor the incredible gift it was for them.

In such moments *receiving the gift actually becomes the service* to one's host. It is the essential habit of mutuality at the core of the life-giving community: "No church entered into partnership with me in giving and receiving except you only" (Phil. 4:15, RSV).

## Homesickness and Homecoming

Three contemporary examples offer hope that established churches can welcome honest seekers, allowing hospitality to flow both ways.

Nora Gallagher, who has reported for *Time* and *Life* and the *New York Times Magazine*, stumbled onto Trinity Episcopal Church in Santa Barbara, California, after years of finding church irrelevant. Her subsequent involvement in the spiritual life of this parish and its social ministries is nothing short of a miracle as reported in her best-selling book, *Things Seen and Unseen: A Year Lived in Faith.* "The Church has taught us what to believe but not how to believe—how to connect our faith with our daily lives," says Canon Lauren Artress in an interview with Gallagher.[66] Here is the charter for reaching tomorrow's seekers. Gallagher has learned to pray in ordinary crises: conflictual vestry meetings, caring for her dying brother, coordinating a homeless shelter, or encountering city officials and social agencies. Her renewed faith becomes the source of energy in the fast-paced liturgies of her life as she offers hospitality to the world's marginalized seekers through her writing.

Charles ("Chuck") Colson wrote *Born Again* in the aftermath of his repentance and imprisonment for his involvement with the Watergate scandal of the Nixon administration. Many skeptics viewed Colson's conversion as "foxhole religion," holding onto a privatized Jesus just to get Colson out of trouble. Thank God, many believing Christians did *not* dismiss Colson but rather nurtured and believed him into new life in community. Today Colson has integrated personal transformation with social transformation, becoming a champion for prison reform with political and social justice.

In *Traveling Mercies,* Anne Lamott tells of her rearing in an atheistic home and her stumbling through drugs, alcohol, and abortion into believing in God in a college class while Kierkegaard's *Fear and Trembling* was being read aloud. But her journey of abuse continued until she experienced *in the solitude of her bedroom* something that seemed like the presence of Jesus, following her around for days like a cat. "But I knew what would happen: you let a cat in one time, give it a little milk, and then it stays forever." That is just what happened: She said yes to Jesus. She went to an Episcopal priest who helped interpret her experience, but she did not join his church. Later, through the simple miracle of being near a flea market, tiny St. Andrew Presbyterian Church drew her into authentic Christian community. She writes of Veronica, a tall African American pastor who sings from the pulpit and tells stories, like this one:

> When she was about seven, her best friend got lost one day. The little girl ran up and down the streets of the big town where they lived, but she couldn't find a single landmark. She was very frightened. Finally a policeman stopped to help her. He put her in the passenger seat of his car, and they drove around until she finally saw her church. She pointed it out to the policeman, and then she told him firmly, "You could let me out now. This is my church, and I can always find my home from here."

"And that is why I have stayed so close to mine—because no matter how bad I am feeling, how lost or lonely or frightened, when I see the faces of the people at my church, and hear their tawny voices, I can always find my way home."[67]

Everyone is homesick. From Thomas Wolfe's *You Can't Go Home Again* to Anne Tyler's *Dinner at the Homesick Restaurant,* homesickness and homecoming are at once ancient yet contemporary metaphors of sin and salvation, repentance and faith. Russell Chandler draws on these images in *Feeding the Flock: Restaurants and Churches You'd Stand in Line For.*[68] Repentance is an acute God-sickness, turning toward the One who yearns for you. Faith begins with believing in God, but its end is trusting that God believes in you.

The gospel of homesickness and homecoming will "preach well" in a global village where younger and older generations feel increasingly estranged by geography, divorce, lifestyle, and vocation—many adults do not understand the highly specialized work their children do. Coming home to God is to know you are understood and loved beyond these barriers of distance, circumstance, and reason—and are received into a new kind of family.

### Welcoming a Generation of Seekers

A renewing urban church prints this message on its picture postcard:

> *Our community is open to all seekers and believers, to growth and questions, to commitment and passion, to service and to witness. Join us.*

Today's old-age or new-age seeker may *begin* the spiritual journey solely as a personal way to survive or as a last resort to find some new kicks after the failure of drugs and alcohol, sex, or success. Sadly, unlike Anne Lamott, many individuals who experience God on their own do *not* experience the church's "welcome home." Many of these secular mystics are very socially conscious and are quick to criticize the church's blind side. Yet *we* criticize them for their private theology! Churches can take the first step toward seekers by doing an examen to see if our walk matches our talk: Try a simple calendar "examen."

> ◆ **Calendar Awareness Prayer (LL 52)** In a group context, ask each person to take a monthly church calendar. Pray for awareness. Then ask the group to mark with a red pen each event primarily aimed at church members with an *M,* using a different color pen to mark those events mainly for people outside the church with an *O.* Afterward, prayerfully reflect together. What is the relationship between the *Ms* and *Os?* What is the invitation for your church?[69]

How can we be a link for seekers to find authentic community unless our own community is authentic? We have a model: Today's seekers are akin to the "God-fearers" in the book of Acts, who spiritually hungered for good news.

*Authentic community begins with contemplation.* I have noticed three things in this regard. First, the seeker often has experienced some spiritual abuse, often in the name of God or the church, that served to "inoculate" the person against institutional Christianity; this calls for bridge-building and unlearning for seeker and guides alike. Second, "pop spirituality"—inside or outside Christendom—is a judgment on established churches. As Dwight L. Moody reportedly said of those who criticized his methods for reaching people off the street, "I like the way I'm doing it better than the way you're not doing it." Third, if we begin by earning the right to be heard and establishing relationships, *we will find many born-again and new-age seekers are actually starving for authentic community and healthy ways to connect with the hurts of the world.*

## Playful Projects for Serious Purpose

Devastating earthquakes in Turkey, Greece, Taiwan, and Mexico have been much in the news as I write. I am fascinated to learn how trained dogs can go into the rubble to sniff out and rescue humans. This training all begins as simple play, like hide-and-go-seek: Dogs are tricked to go behind certain trees. If they find human beings there they are rewarded—no humans, no reward. I recall a third-hand phrase I heard somewhere: "playful projects for serious purposes."

What occurs to me is the simplicity and playfulness of this training for the most ultimately serious purpose of rescuing death-trapped human beings. Recently, a student who is blind told how her dog Jazz was involved in the 1995 Oklahoma City bombing rescue project and how play sessions had to be scheduled to renew the dogs' spirits when they became discouraged.

Hospitality as a sabbath practice is serious yet playful. In rabbinic tradition the sabbath is a day "to play and to pray." In Luke's Gospel Jesus is continually playing, often on the sabbath. On his way to a party, inviting himself to one, on his way home from one, he plays with words as he tells about them, yet all for the most serious purpose: the soul's relationship with God and neighbor.

Many seekers begin the spiritual journey playfully, *loving self (or yearning to) and the world for the self's sake,* to paraphrase Bernard of Clairvaux. But it becomes our task to entertain these pleasure seekers as angels unawares (God speaking to us through them), because in time of crisis they may begin *loving God, even if it is for the self's sake,* to get out of trouble or protect their self-image. Worship is a movement *from* entertaining angels unawares to involving them!—till they move to *loving God for God's sake.* Finally the goal is to return to *loving self and the world again, but now for God's sake.*

But this is not a case of "them" and "us." This is our own journey too, helplessly falling in love with self and the world ultimately in order to fall in love with God in the world. The four movements mentioned above are the essence of hospitality—we can extend no genuine hospitality to the world until we experience divine hospitality for ourselves in the world: "You are precious in my sight, and honored, and I love you" (Isa. 43:4).

One way to begin closing the "them and us" gap is through creative and contemplative intercessory prayer. The next time you walk beside a person outside your normal boundary of relationships, think of your walking as a prayer to walk in that person's shoes. Consider hosting your church committee meetings in a room or site that becomes "Meeting Space as Intercession" (Resource VI.). Next time someone from another continent comes to mind as you drive or do dishes, think of your awareness of that person as already a prayer. *Being* with others by proxy makes a difference in the quality of our *doing* in person.

WESTERN REFLECTION

I will not try to speak as Indian,
African, Latin American, or Asian.
Instead I will reflect as Western
and as Christian which is what I am.

Would we had never tried to give alone
but mutually receive and live as one—
a love to share, a hope to dare,
a truth to find while being found.

And can it be that I should gain
an interest in my neighbor's pain—
yet in the same encounter learn
the secret path for which I yearn?

—Kent Ira Groff © 1999

Such inward hospitality for the shamed and shaming aspects of my own self is the essence of Jesus' extending the forgiveness of sins to the prostituting, tax collecting, prodigal part of my own soul. Yet, though charity may begin at home (loving self), it can never end there and stay alive. As Maria Harris writes in *Proclaim Jubilee!: A Spirituality for the Twenty-First Century,* "The work that returns us home will often send us far away."[70] And it is that faraway place that the soul of outreach yearns to explore while simultaneously coming home to self.

## 2. Prayer as Global Awareness

The model prayer that Jesus gave the community becomes our guide in two respects. First, it begins as a prayer for global awareness: "Our Father in heaven, hallowed be your name, your kingdom come, your will be done, *on earth as it is in heaven....*" Second, it is in the plural (*Our* father.... Give *us*...; forgive *us* as *we* forgive). This awareness can be called "glocal" awareness— both global and local. Meister Eckhart said, "There is no such things as *my* bread, only *our* bread." Only in community can I become aware of Christ's presence *in* the world's pain; alone I will remain unaware and be swallowed up by its pain.

My plane had just arrived in Calcutta. Seated for only moments in one of the ambulances of Mother Teresa's Missionaries of Charity, I was handed a letter inviting me to give a lecture at Morning Star Regional Seminary in Barrackpore during the week of prayer for Christian unity. I thought, *What are the crucial issues that threaten to divide us? East from West? Christians from one another? from the rest of the world?*

With only forty-eight hours to prepare, my mind immediately was drawn back to Kirkridge retreat center in Bangor, Pennsylvania, where one afternoon some of us had been playing an educational board game. The question I drew was this: What is the greatest problem as we face the twenty-first century? The problem I chose at that time—*the widening gap between poor and rich people*—became the first issue for my lecture. Even in so short a time in Calcutta I saw unspeakable poverty.

When I arrived at the retreat center where I would stay, this news headline greeted me: "Australian Missionary and Two Sons Burned to Death in Car." In India, Israel, Ireland, Iran, and Iraq—all around the world—"fundamentalist" extremists persecute believers and one another. Here was my second issue: *the uniqueness and the universality of Christ in a pluralistic world.* The martyred missionary was Graham Staines, who with his wife Gladys was living out the gospel by creating a Christian community for rejected lepers. (As I write this several months later, a *New York Times* headline reads, "Murdered Missionary's Widow Returns to Work with India's Lepers.") Such devotion was the third crucial issue: *the unity of spirituality and action.*

### Awareness: Three Crucial Issues for Tomorrow's Church[71]

"God so loved the *world*...that *whoever* believes..." (John 3:16, RSV). Here is the mandate for the twenty-first century as for the first-century church: to balance the "world" with the "whoever"—a personal gospel for a global context. The context is not far away in so-called developing countries; it is also in the so-called "developed" countries, with people of color in Germany, Britain, the U.S., Canada, and Koreans in Latin America. Native Americans are the fastest-growing minority in the U.S.; Chinese is the third most spoken language in Canada, next to English and French. The irony is that while the *economic* gap is widening, the *geographical* gap is shrinking—so poverty and racism are now "in your face," on your own street, in your own family.

A single theme runs through the whole Bible: "Listen to Love, to love." Dietrich Bonhoeffer wrote, "The first service that one renders to the community is that of listening to one's brother and sister." "'Listen to me, O coastlands, pay attention, you peoples from far away!' And [God] said to me, 'You are my servant'" (Isa. 49:1, 3). Serving begins with contemplative listening.

These three issues command our prayerful listening to pay attention to the cry of God's love and to the cries of the world simultaneously. To split any of these categories (poor from rich, the unique Christ from universal love, prayer from action) is to lose the integrity of the gospel and the unity of the church. It is to threaten the humanity of the planet and one's very soul.

1. *The widening gap between poor and rich people* is the greatest cause of division between northern and southern hemisphere nations, within every denomination and each local church. A 1999 United Nations report on the widening gap says the combined wealth of the world's three richest families is greater than the annual income of 600 million people in the least-developed countries. A computer would cost the average Bangladeshi eight years' income, while the average American would pay one month's wage.

How do I as a member of the world's wealthiest nation dare to proclaim this message? To "listen to Love, to love" is to become a servant to the poor by listening simultaneously to the cries of the least of these, to the cry of God—and to the cry of my own needy soul. It is good for us who are materially privileged to realize that materially poor people actually can be more "advanced" than ourselves. For example, among impoverished village families in poor nations, people often speak five or six languages and have highly developed spiritual and intellectual insights. It becomes clear in comparison that we who are materially rich are linguistically and spiritually needy.

An important way to begin to close this gap is to encourage more cross-cultural exchanges and church partnerships. As in the seminary where I teach, we need to offer such programs as part of the curriculum in training pastors and lay ministers. A seventeen-year-old was radically changed by going to Malawi in Africa and later served in Ecuador and Kenya. She now focuses on providing health care for poor women in a mountainous area of the U.S.

The gap expands. Advances in science, technology, and genetic engineering threaten to make their benefits even less available to the twenty-first century poor. Violence against Christians and other devout people is increasing, especially *among* poor groups themselves, as in Rwanda, the Sudan, the Balkans. Yet we are called to join Christ, who "has broken down the dividing wall, that is, the hostility between us" (Eph. 2:14). We can begin with a simple step of praying to make friends across cultural lines: tutoring English as a second language where we live, sponsoring a child abroad, working with illegal aliens or imprisoned refugees. By creating cross-cultural experiences we join the risen Christ in breaking down the dividing walls. Mother Teresa was right: "We can do no great things, only small things with great love."

Believers returning from cross-cultural experiences at home or abroad begin to appreciate the risk of confessing Christ and loving enemies. We begin to notice the needs of others in our own communities, to continue ties to other cultures, and to value the neediness of our own soul instead of stuffing it with more materialism. The efforts of a single individual can be miraculously multiplied, like the meager loaves and fishes in Christ's hands, by being part of secular and church organizations that work for peace and justice and the transformation of political, scientific, and medical structures. The words of Margaret Mead embody a prophetic truth: "Never doubt that a small group of thoughtful, committed citizens can change the world; indeed, it's the only thing that ever has."

*2. The uniqueness and universality of Christ* is the second key issue in an increasingly pluralistic world. To paraphrase John's Gospel, this is the good news: "For God so loved the world (universal) that God gave the only (unique) Son" *so that each human being may become the unique daughter or son of God that she or he is intended to be—and begin to experience eternal life now!* Some Christians so emphasize the *uniqueness* of their own understanding of Christ that they alienate people of other religions and allow no dialogue, even with Christians different from themselves. Others so emphasize the *universality* of divine love that they lose the particularity of Christ. How can we keep these two themes together in a dynamic tension, as they are in this most-quoted text of John 3:16?

It is possible to see the uniqueness of Jesus' cross and resurrection as a universal theme in all human experience: "The world breaks everyone and afterward many are strong at the broken places," wrote Ernest Hemingway in *A Farewell to Arms.* Here is the universal theme of brokenness that is experienced by everyone—rich and poor, humanist and agnostic, Christian, Jew, Hindu, Muslim and Buddhist, Zoroastrian. "And afterward many are strong at the broken places." Whenever the human spirit springs back with love out of tragedy, wherever natural disasters are transformed into beauty and new life, there is the hidden wholeness, the Christ *incognito*—as on the way to Emmaus (Luke 24:13-35).

This unique paschal mystery of the crucified-rising Christ embodies a universal theme: Brokenness is transformed to blessing. The world is filled with Eucharist! Evangelism is calling people "to turn around" ("repent"—*metanoia* in Greek) and offer their shame and brokenness as the source of their greatest gift to the community. It is the mystery hidden for ages—"which is Christ in you, the hope of glory" (Col. 1:27).

When one of my daughters was about three years old we were driving by a lake one night when she asked, "Why is the moon always following us?" Congratulating her for a wonderful question, I remember telling her that even if there were a thousand cars driving by and a million people standing on the shore, each would see the moonbeam aimed directly at his or her own feet. Something in the mystery of light makes it so. The story illustrates that the more we connect with particular persons and cultures, the more we can have confidence that the uniqueness of Christ's love will emerge in the context of every individual and culture. Loss of soul in our time has to do with losing this confidence.

The analogy can be continued: Jesus says, "I am the light of the world" (John 8:12). Like light, which physicists tell us is paradoxically both a "particle" and a "wave," Jesus was a particular Jew who lived in the first century, yet through the resurrection, has refracted in a wavelike manner throughout the world: "I am the light of the world." Jesus also said, "You are the light of the world" (Matt. 5:14). The uniqueness of Jesus calls us to affirm the genetic and experiential particulars of each person we encounter, yet also to discover our wave-like resonance common to all humankind. The more we become light, the more we participate in the unique gifts and pain of others and experience oneness with all peoples of the world—sharing the sufferings and joy of Christ.

When we listen to people's faith stories, we will undoubtedly hear in them places of pain and impasse, places of joy and insight. When this happens, we are standing on holy ground.

3. **The unity of spirituality and action** is the message of the Incarnation: "the Word became flesh" (John 1:14). Yet the split between these two divides churches and peoples in every land—those who favor prayer, those who favor social action. Mother Teresa embodied this unity of spiritual and physical—*and hers was never coercive evangelism.* In every center of the Missionaries of Charity is a chapel with the crucifix with Christ's words: "I thirst." To quench the thirst of Jesus in the lives of the poor is to quench our own thirst for divine love. African American spirituals convey this essential unity of the spiritual and social: "Swing low, sweet chariot, coming for to carry me home" is at once a song about going to heaven and a call to political liberation from any form of enslavement. This union is what W. E. B. Du Bois in *The Souls of Black Folk* meant by "the Sorrow Songs":

Through all the sorrow of the Sorrow Songs there breathes a hope—
a faith in the ultimate justice of things. The minor cadences of
despair change often to triumph and calm confidence. Sometimes it
is faith in life, sometimes a faith in death, sometimes assurance of
boundless justice in some fair world beyond.[72]

But always the hope is clear: for a world where heaven and earth converge—as in icons of the Orthodox church where gold and earth colors meet—
for a union of prayer and action. "Your will be done on earth as it is in heaven."

Sandhya was the first woman to be ordained in the Church of North India,
serving as copastor with her husband. Word was out among some that "if that
woman celebrates Communion, we're not coming forward to receive." She
waited and prayed for a whole year; then the Sunday came when the clergy
couple and a few trusted members thought the time was right. Picture the
scene. As Sandhya lifted the bread in the liturgy that morning, it was at once
a union of the holiest prayers of the church and a radical political action on
behalf of the dignity of women. And the people came. This was true liturgy,
"a celebration of God's work in the people's lives."

The route from a disembodied spirituality to a hands-on connection with the
world is always through community. We cannot communicate that Christ is
the bread of life to someone who has no bread. The question is not whether
we believe in evangelism or social action, but whether our deeds proclaim the
unique and universal message of Jesus. In words attributed to Saint Francis
of Assisi, "Preach the gospel at all times; if necessary use words."

We become an apostolic community, being sent into the world and also
co-missioning others.

> ◞ **Rituals of Sending (LL 53)** Every form of good-bye—little leav-
> ings and the final dying to new life—is a ripe opportunity for
> rituals of commissioning, the meaning of *apostolé*, "one who is
> sent forth." Offer the option to folks who leave for service proj-
> ects, for work in a different state, for new vocations at home—for
> blessing in corporate worship or small groups. (A few leaders lay
> hands on the one(s) leaving, inviting the *entire congregation* to
> place hands on the shoulders of others standing near them in the
> pews while joining in prayer.)

## Prayer and Action: Contemplation and Manifestation

Quakers speak of the ideal unity of prayer and action, as Douglas Steere wrote in *Work and Contemplation*:

> For there is a point where, blasphemous as it may sound, the con-
> templator is always at prayer and where [one] is free to carry [one's]
> action into the contemplation and the contemplation into the
> action....It is, in short, *an abiding disposition*, and out of this the
> works come.[73]

The goal of Christian maturity is not spiritual schizophrenia—a seesaw between prayer and action. Rather the goal is for the spaces between prayer and action to grow ever closer and closer, until a paradoxical union is created, like the wave-particle mystery of light. A beautiful Celtic prayer poem in Esther de Waal's *God Under My Roof* represents this union. Most likely it is the prayer of a woman who is lighting a fire in the hearth—simultaneously praying for God to light a flame of love in her heart:

> I will kindle my fire this morning
> In the presence of the holy angels of heaven,
> In the presence of Ariel of the loveliest form,
> In the presence of Uriel of the myriad charms,
> Without malice, without jealousy, without envy,
> Without fear, without terror of anyone under the sun,
> But the Holy Son of God to shield me.
>> Without malice, without jealousy, without envy,
>> Without fear, without terror of anyone under the sun,
>> But the Holy Son of God to shield me
>
> God, kindle Thou in my heart within
> A flame of love to my neighbor,
> To my foe, to my friend, to my kindred all,
> To the brave, to the knave, to the thrall,
> O Son of the loveliest Mary,
> From the lowliest thing that liveth
> To the name that is highest of all.

Karl Marx observed modern people's increasing alienation from their work. Yet the ancient Celts prayed with rocks and fire and water, the elements of their work, with no separation. Can we learn to pray with our work—with microwaves and computers that are the products of nature, and in the marketplace of technology? If not, are we hopelessly condemned to deny the very faith we profess, and to destroy the very unity of a world that is at once sacred and secular? Can we not baptize the "cyber" along with the "space" to embrace a "cyberspace" leadership style that values spaciousness in the liturgies of our lives?

A decade ago I was trying desperately to print out a professional paper to present to a group; I had less than half an hour to print and copy it and arrive. The system jammed, of course. I tried everything. In panic, I realized I was kneeling at eye level with the computer, keyboard, external disk, and monitor. I shut each piece down completely: off. I was left for seconds on my knees, waiting to boot up, and in that moment I relinquished the whole project. I was the one needing to shut down my own stressed, internal computers—a self-emptying *kenosis*, a sabbath moment. I was free again. As I rebooted, everything printed. But I learned that we can pray with technology or allow it to become a prayer—not unlike the Celts with stubborn cows, felled trees, and frozen rivers. I do not wait for the next frozen computer.

When *being* and *doing* converge, then we can "be doing" Christ's work in every experience of life. Both are prayer: One is prayer of contemplation, the other prayer of manifestation. As Dietrich Bonhoeffer wrote in his *Letters and Papers from Prison*, "Our being Christians today will be limited to two things: prayer and righteous action among people. All Christian thinking, speaking, and organizing must be born anew out of this prayer and action." The spiritual life is continually discerning, How can these two come together?

## 3. Discerning Vision—and Outreach

I met Kevin, a physician-professor at Johns Hopkins University, at Princeton Theological Seminary in a seminar I was leading on the Quaker practice of a Clearness Committee. (See LL 50.) He had come to discern whether to leave medicine and attend seminary.

When the group focused on Kevin's concern, this story unfolded. He had served as a volunteer doctor in Haiti, in a cross-cultural mission trip sponsored by his denomination. Noting no scheduled times for daily worship or reflection, he thought it strange for a church-sponsored group. He spoke to the leader who explained that their purpose was social service— and besides, one participant was Jewish. One evening Kevin announced that if anyone would like to reflect on the adventures of the day and pray, he would be sitting on a certain brick wall at 7:00 P.M. Nearly everyone came, the first being the Jewish participant! In a natural and joyous way, these meetings continued nightly with stories, singing, silence, and prayer.

Our group listened as Kevin sensed their affirmation: He had used his spiritual *and* his medical gifts. After three days, he concluded that he was already in ministry. He has since been back to Haiti, to Bolivia—and to Uganda, where, as a nonordained Christian, he was invited to speak before thousands of Muslims in the context of authentic service.

In Kevin's story we see that discerning our vocation does not happen in a spiritual vacuum. Simple involvement in the work we feel called to do—and communal reflection on that action—is a more biblical mode of discerning God's intention for our complex lives. Present your bodies in action, sacrifice in worship; and let your minds be renewed "that you may discern what is the will of God" (Rom. 12:2).

## 4. A Paradigm Story: Peter and Cornelius

Giving without receiving is always a downward gesture, and it is the dangerous temptation of the spiritual life and the downside of the missionary movement to act out of a subtly superior position, unconsciously treating the other as an inferior. Cultivating the Eastern tradition of "one hand receiving, the other hand giving" is essential to any evangelical outreach with integrity. We see this reciprocity in Jesus' encounter with the Canaanite woman: A mutual change occurs as the insider-outsider boundary is redrawn (Matt. 15:21-28).

In the key paradigm shift of the early church, *both* Peter *and* Cornelius are changed in their encounter (Acts 10). The story begins simply: Peter goes upstairs to pray. In a dream, God uses simple table etiquette regarding acceptable foods to open Peter's limited perspective: "God has shown me that I should not call anyone profane or unclean." Peter's "conversion" is integral to conversion of the Gentile military officer Cornelius—who then chooses to embrace the radical Way of a Jewish pacifist sect and a rival lord to Caesar!

Hospitality starts inside one's own little self, then opens one to a radical hospitality of God who includes others outside one's circle. Peter's conversion through a dream in solitude breaks open the community to a dream that includes the whole world. I once heard Leslie Newbegin, former bishop of the Church of South India, state a powerful truth while commenting on this story: *The mark of genuine evangelism is when both parties are changed in the encounter.*

◆ **Cross-Cultural Friendship (LL 54)** Read the text of John 15:12-15 about servants and friends. Use the personal or group *lectio* (Resource I or II) to pray with this text, being particularly attentive to a person or group of persons different from yourself to whom you feel drawn in friendship. Spend some time meditating and praying for yourself and the other(s). If ideas come to you during the praying, jot them down in your journal. Then put everything aside. Spend some time in silent contemplation, knowing that you and the other(s) are known and loved by God. Idea: Put a sticky note a few pages ahead in your journal jotting a reminder to ask yourself, How am I praying for (*name or concern*)?

## Evangelism from Below: Beggars Showing Beggars

To make friends across the barriers of your own faith circle is the gift and challenge of *evangelism*—a word better defined as faith finding, faith sharing. This calls for trust in the Spirit for guidance to know when to speak of our experiences of God, when to be silent, and when to let one's actions speak.

Faith sharing can only be meaningful in a context of continued faith finding in our own experiences of doubt and celebration. Genuine hospitality shares the gospel from below: one beggar showing another beggar glimpses of grace in the grit.

This understanding provides the lens for any meaningful contact with seekers and visitors who cross our paths. In the last parish I served, we involved many "priests" in new-member hospitality. A retired member tabulated the "friendship pads" on Monday mornings and passed on names of visitors to a trained volunteer deacon, who, early that same week, made welcoming phone calls—often rich conversations. Later a pastor (or a lay team) set up appointments and visited those who expressed interest—in their homes, businesses, or a neutral lunch spot. Each received a personal invitation (by letter and sometimes by phone) to an inquirer's orientation several times a year and continued receiving many reinvitations and the church newsletter.

Formal pastoral calls are not part of the current lifestyle of the young generation. Yet in a strange way, that fact creates a hunger for intimacy within boundaries—the principle of "high-tech, high-touch." Given an opportunity to share one-to-one, many will discuss personal areas they would not readily share in a small-group context. Ben Campbell Johnson's book title is instructive—many yearn for genuine *Speaking of God: Evangelism as Initial Spiritual Guidance*. A biblical model for this kind of intimacy is the story of

Philip's interpreting the text of Isaiah to the marginalized Ethiopian eunuch (Acts 8:26-40).

- **Liturgical Hospitality (LL 55)** Crucial to genuine witness as hospitality are the many gestures that communicate a welcoming atmosphere in the worshiping community. Assess your own service of worship in the light of these themes of hospitality: an inviting ethos, clearly marked signs, a welcoming and well-staffed nursery, avoidance of in-house language (like groups listed by alphabetical acronyms), worship cues (LL 3) to interpret liturgical gestures or frequently used phrases.

- **Bread for Visitors (LL 56)** Some churches keep a supply of fresh frozen bread, replenished each month. On Sundays loaves are thawed, baked, and given to visitors during worship (or delivered to their homes later that day) as a sign of hospitality— a wonder-filled gesture that communicates the essence of being church.

- **One-to-One Welcoming (LL 57)** Pray. Consider training one or two volunteers to phone visitors to your church, using friendship pads—and using discretion, inquiring if the person has a church home. (Do not discount relatives attending baptisms and such events; they are often churchless.) For introverts threatened by groups and put off by impersonal institutions, *merely the offer for a low-key visit by a pastor or lay team may itself bear the fruit of love.*

- **Community Welcoming (LL 58)** At five- or six-week intervals, invite recent visitors and other "friends" of the church to dinner at the home of a leader or pastor or at the church—hosted by the membership team. Invite other church officers and members involved in mission projects. This model establishes at the outset that spirituality is embodied hospitality in community. (This event is separate from membership classes.) Also encourage all members to invite visitors, neighbors, and one another to break bread in homes or restaurants.

Garnett E. Foster of Tacoma Park Presbyterian Church in Maryland writes of the value of this practice of "Community Welcoming" mentioned above: "Each dinner event has taken on a personality of its own. Something unique happens as people gather around the table. Often international people are included. Many of them have commented that it is the first time they have been invited into an American home—a painful reflection of our culture for those of us who have known hospitality during travel."[74]

⮞ **Action Welcoming (LL 59)** Invite nonmembers to participate in training projects in church and service projects outside church. This kind of reverse hospitality is suited to today's seekers—finding communion with God by becoming part of community. Welcome their expertise working with Habitat for Humanity or in the soup kitchen—singing in the choir, carpentering, caregiving, educating, drumming, or dancing even before they join.

These methods of faith finding and faith sharing create laboratory experiments in grace. The Acts of the Apostles and Paul's letters clearly show that the earliest believers continually experimented with grace. Try some one-to-one methods, some community methods, some action methods, some of all kinds—praying to discern how to "listen to Love, to love" in your context. But do not try any of them without praying. Learning from failed or foiled experiences will deepen radical trust in the Spirit and vulnerable love in community.

### DOING GOOD NEWS

How do you share Good
News?
How do you spread
Light?
   Make friends.
   Do good.
   Break bread.
Risk and pray till others ask
the Source.

Matthew 5:14-16
—**Kent Ira Groff** © 1999

## 5. Silent Presence: Salt and Light

Two primary images for the community of Jesus' followers reflect silent presence: "You are the salt of the earth" and "You are the light of the world" (Matt. 5:13-16). In primal cultures salt is a preservative; it speaks of a silent, invisible presence, of keeping things from disintegrating, of adding zest. In a Mediterranean restaurant I enjoyed delicious fish broiled in layers of salt—yet the fish did not taste salty, only more flavorful. Likewise, light has this same silent, invisible quality—enhancing the unique features of the objects it lights up, though never visible in itself.

Yet in the same verses Jesus warns against the salt losing its flavor, against putting the light under a basket. Each is to be spread out into the world—proclaiming God's presence. Light and salt speak of abundance out of scarcity, or presence through silence. Walter Brueggemann writes of "the liturgy of abundance, the myth of scarcity":

> Wouldn't it be wonderful if liberal and conservative churchpeople, who love to quarrel with each other, came to a common realization that the real issue confronting us is whether the news of God's abundance can be trusted in the face of the story of scarcity?[25]

A friend returning from China recounts recent church history there. When the U.S. and China fought each other in the Korean Conflict, all Western missionaries had to leave China in 1951. Many thought the church in China would die. Instead, as in Korea and other Asian countries, Chinese believers adopted the "three self" way of being church: self-governing, self-supporting, and self-propagating. The absence of Western leaders became a goad for indigenous spiritual development.

From 1966 to 1976 during the Cultural Revolution under Mao, Chinese Christians had to go underground, yet grew incredibly, silently. Their seasoned character preserved them. Now once again their lights can shine more freely. Though only one to two percent of the population, Chinese Christians grew from 750,000 in 1949 to an estimated 12,000,000 Protestant believers alone. Outward scarcity can be a goad to multiply spiritual intelligences.

When *linguistic* and *logical* communications are snuffed out, the soul of church continues with greater dependence on other means: creative use of *space*, like house churches; *music* that implants faith in the heart; *gestures* of liturgy and hospitality; deepened *interpersonal* community and *intrapersonal* solitude; and ways of seeing God in the cathedrals of *nature* when human cathedrals are closed.

As in China, today in India and in many African, Asian, and Latin American countries, the spoken or printed word is often suppressed—yet the Christian community's salty fervor and flavor continues. Our whole idea of what makes for success is often turned upside down when we examine powerful deeds of God in the biographies of reformers of our own faith communities. One sees the *kenosis* of Jesus Christ in Ron Ellsberg's *All Saints: Daily Reflections on Saints, Prophets, and Witnesses for Our Time*—disciples like Dorothy Day and Vincent van Gogh who emptied their own plans and projects, surprised by joy in sacrifice.

A woman at a retreat gave me a wholly deeper understanding of the discipline of solitude. She queried, "I think I've experienced the discipline of solitude by hanging in there with group after group where I've felt like the odd person out—yet somehow my presence was necessary, even though the aloneness in community was intense." She had explained my entire life to me, I told her; I experienced the true moment of hospitality where student became teacher. She expressed Paul's counter-cultural advice: "Do not be conformed to the world, but be transformed."

A "failed" mission experience can be a laboratory of spiritual learning. In *The Active Life*, Parker Palmer tells of being asked to serve as a sociologist to consult with a suburban church that had entered into a partner relationship with a church in an inner city area. The suburban church had experienced nothing but frustration. Church members felt their efforts to relate to the other church were not working, even though the two churches had tried to work on mutual goals and avoid paternalism. During the course of the meeting, the insight began to dawn on the group that this very experience of powerlessness might be as close as these privileged Anglo-Saxon folks could ever get to the daily feelings of frustration and helplessness of their sisters and brothers in the city congregation. In a reverse kind of way, this spiritual impasse had become the beginning of inter-institutional healing and intrapersonal learning.[76]

While working on my lawn I heard a song on the radio: "You Can't Always Get What You Want." The line would not leave me, and as I continued to work I realized the reverse was also true: "You can't always give what you want." When you can't always *give* what you want and when your help is rejected, your ego is bruised—and you can't *get* the recognition you wanted. What you want may even be for a good cause, like bridging the widening gap.

## Creating Individual and Institutional Integrity

Both Testaments of the Bible make it clear that that a sharp rift between rich and poor is not in accord with God's design. But where to begin—or begin again? I can start by noticing the needy aspects of my own soul and by inviting the shamed and shaming parts of myself to the table of the Lord. I can pray for awareness of others not in my circle. When I pray, amazingly I discover right in my own community persons whose gifts have been shunned or ignored. I can make an effort to invite their gifts into the circles of my life through table conversations, small groups, outreach projects, and worship.

Then I can pray for the circle to widen. Within my own organization we are only beginning. Inclusiveness must occur at five levels simultaneously: at the level of the board, the staff, the participants, the curriculum resources, and probably most difficult—the intrapersonal level. If I had to isolate one, it would be the intrapersonal, since doing my inner homework affects all the rest of my work. I have learned that variety in my music and reading is a key, along with ongoing prayer for such connections. That homework is never done, so diving right into working relationships with others different from myself is part of my inner training. I struggle not only with the barriers created by race—but of economics, denominational theologies, generational styles, learning differences, sexual orientation, musical tastes, and physical and emotional distinctions. I am always praying for my soul's integrity to reflect the embracing arc of God's Spirit as I see it reflected in Jesus.

> ➴ **Discerning Multicultural Community (LL 60)** Work and pray for God's institutional hospitality at five levels—board, staff, participants, curriculum, and, most difficult, the intrapersonal level. Begin by praying to make friends outside your circle—by expanding your reading, travel, music, and entertainment.

I am learning that this kind of hospitality keeps me praying on a razor's edge, my heart continually lifted to God in gratitude for tiny glimpses of the God's "kindom"—this new family— on earth, that instead of rejecting another I may discover there a hidden part of myself to be embraced and loved again. To create friendship with persons outside my own comfort zone is a good way of "meeting Jesus again for the first time."

# Postlude

## Finding Spiritual Direction in Ministry

I hope each leader in tomorrow's church will meet regularly with a spiritual mentor or director *and* will also serve as one for another leader or leader in training, for youth or adult seekers or members. This will accomplish two things. First, it keeps us honest before God. How dare I meet with a thirsty soul on Tuesday if I have not met with God on Monday? Second, by focusing intently on traces of grace in a few individuals' lives, we find spiritual direction happening "on the run" with many—at the water cooler, over lunch, in a classroom. Men especially relate to impromptu spiritual care. And women especially benefit from relational spirituality. This one-to-one art of spiritual friendship is as ancient as Ruth and Naomi, David and Jonathan, Jesus and the Beloved Disciple. In addition, either find or found a spiritual support group for yourself. I say this to all—lay *and* clergy ministers.

During a concert intermission, I was conversing with a lay leader who had served several times in the highest position on his local church board, as well as national levels of his denomination. "You'll be interested to know that I finally felt healed enough to go back on my church board." Twice he mentioned being "healed enough"—ten years after the third devastating pastoral crisis in that congregation.

In the space of two days four pastors told me of the following incidents that had triggered major church conflicts: an advent wreath, a worn-out typewriter given in memory of a church member, an usher dressed in casual clothes, and a minister's hug of a church member in public. A spiritual guide might ask, "How are you praying in relation to all of this? in relation to the small stuff as well as the big issues?" The little things can do us in—but God is in the details. So the spiritual guide would then ask, "What might God be wanting to say to you beneath the incident?"

Lay Christians as well as pastors are being deeply wounded. I wrote this book because I believe three things passionately. First, the very soul of the body of Christ is threatened by these insidious conflicts; second, organizational development strategies are only effective if there is a spiritual base for life together; and third, books and seminars that "enlighten" clergy without lay leaders often escalate conflict.

Here I have offered spiritual practices that can be used by lay leaders and pastors *together* to renew the soul of the church's ordinary ministries. We need spiritual direction in ministry.

The first thing I want to happen is for leaders to step back and look at the multiple pieces of their lives and their ministries and ask, What holds it all together? The answer is in the gospel pattern of Christ: the rhythms of involvement (ministry functions) and withdrawal (sabbath practices). The stories told here have shown how the mystery of Christ transforms barriers in ministry into transmitters of life-giving passion, integrity and wholeness.

The last thing I want to happen is for church leaders to "import" spiritual practices into their already overprogrammed lives and communities. So I have continually focused on practices to keep church leaders vital in their own faith, which will also leaven their institutional laboratories of faith.

In this way I keep coming back to the first question: What holds it all together? What is God's invitation? in my life? in my faith community? in the world? God, grant me the grace to remember what's important.

As C. S. Lewis said, "The charge is 'Feed my sheep' not 'run experiments on my rats.'"[77] There is a mountain of social-scientific research, and all has its place in determining, for example, how many denominations have lost members since the sixties or how prayer affects health. Yet our faith communities need ways of feeding sheep, being church for one another—the sensing nerves and pulsating muscles and discerning mind of the body of Christ. That is what these laboratory experiments are about.

In Switzerland, after sheep have grazed lush lowlands, they must scale the craggy slopes. The climb is hard, the grazing difficult. Old ewes and rams who have been there before resist. But shepherds have learned that if they pick up the young lambs and carry them, the older sheep will follow because they love their young. This is a parable for the soul of tomorrow's church.

## WEDDING LIGHT

At this glorious wedding
feast of West and East,
shedding Light on Love's best
gifts received and given,
stands shadowed
Mary facing West:
"Your joy is gone,"
she says while always
pointing toward her Son:
"Whatever he tells you
do it." Messiah Jesu
now commands:
"Fill the jars...

Fill the jars with stories
that sparkle with surprise,
the ferment of suspense...
Fill the jars with music,
the rhythms of grace
in drum and dance...
Fill the jars with ordinary
drops of experience,
holy silence,
joy in sacrifice."

This steward
may yet announce,
"You have saved
the best till last!"

John 2:1-11

—Kent Ira Groff © 1999

# Resources
# Bibliography
# Notes
# Index

## RESOURCE I—Praying with Scripture
Personal *Lectio Divina* Process

Many of us think of our personal devotional life as consisting of reading the Bible—then saying our prayers. In this exercise of *praying the scriptures* the two come together. In the fifth century, Benedict gave us a simple method: *lectio divina*—the "divine" or "prayerful" reading of scriptures. Read a short text prayerfully—over and over, like a cow chewing her cud—until you are led to "delight in God." Benedict's *lectio* was later outlined in a fourfold experience, beginning with silence:

1.) *Reading:* like a cow grazing, select and read a brief portion of scripture silently, aloud, or both ways;

2.) *Meditating:* like a cow chewing, reread the scripture, ponder the context—allow meanings and associations to come to mind;

3.) *Praying:* like a cow regurgitating its cud, ruminate on the text; let it get down in your gut and connect with your raw feelings;

4.) *Contemplating:* like the cow resting and digesting, allow the Word you need to get into your bloodstream.

Contemplation is what the psalmist means by "Delight yourself in the Lord and [God] will give you the desires of your heart" (37:4, NIV). It is Luke's image of Mary sitting at the feet of Jesus, listening. Speaking of prayer, John Calvin wrote that Jesus "taught us to seek a retreat that would help us to descend into our heart....God...will be near to us in the affections of our hearts."[78]

When we pray with scripture the Word becomes flesh in us embodied in service. Three options for praying with scripture have been passed down through the centuries:

1.) Use the imagination to visualize a scene in a narrative text.

2.) Converse with the various characters. (Reflect inwardly or by using a journal).

3.) Repeat a short phrase that lures you, like a centering prayer. Keep your journal and Bible with you during personal prayer times.

## RESOURCE II—Scripture Sharing
### Group *Lectio Divina* Process

This method comes out of monastic practice where it was called *collatio,* originally "the bringing together" of a shared supper. It is a bringing together of friends and stories and of connections they bring related to a scripture text. Group *lectio* is used in meetings, lunch breaks in work situations, and in "base communities" of developing countries where Bible study, prayer, singing, personal compassion, and social action often merge. This is a unique way to create small group *koinonía* even in a large gathering or space. (Allow a half hour, longer if extending time at Step 3.) Each person needs a Bible or printed text (ten verses maximum).

LEADER OF LARGE GROUP: Briefly summarize the purpose and process; announce the text. Have participants form groups of four to no more than seven (may be in same room); sit in a close circle. Have each group designate a convener.

STEP 1. *Listen for God's word "as it touches your life." Notice a word, phrase, or metaphor that "shimmers"—lures you or unnerves you.*

- ❖ Convener in each small group: Celebrate the presence of Christ, using a brief spoken prayer, a song, or chant. Focus on breathing, followed by silence.
- ❖ Repeat invitation in Step 1 above. Allow silence. Or invite the group to read the text silently first.
- ❖ Read the text aloud slowly to the group; perhaps read it again. *(lectio)*
- ❖ Extend this invitation to each person: "Begin to repeat a word or phrase silently, or visualize a metaphor or an image." Allow a few minutes of quiet. *(meditatio)*
- ❖ Invite persons to share a word, phrase, or metaphor that touches their life *without commenting on it.*

STEP 2. *Notice some feeling or experience in relation to the word, phrase, or metaphor.* (*oratio*—prayer)

- ❖ SECOND READING: The convener (or another person) reads the text aloud again, slowly.
- ❖ Invite (don't insist!) each person to share a second time, *reflecting on some feeling or experience.*

  (Accept sharing, usually without discussion; use *I, me*—avoid *we, us, you*; keep confidentiality; be comfortable with silence; listen attentively, receiving another's experience as a gift.)

**STEP 3.** Invite persons to ask themselves the following questions: *"What is God inviting me to do or be this week? Am I being called to some action—now in this setting, in my relationships with family, church, work, leisure?"*

(Before the third reading, announce whether the group has an extended time, Option A or B, below.)

❖ THIRD READING: The convener (or yet another person) reads the text aloud a third time.

A: Take an extended time to explore these connections via reflection, journaling, art, movement, or other ways of praying. Persons may stay or leave as they are ready, keeping the room area for silence. Announce time to return.

B: Move directly from the third reading (after brief silence) to sharing discoveries, below.

❖ Return to group(s). The convener says, "Let's continue to pray by telling what we've discovered—yearnings and connections, any beckonings to action or decision."

**STEP 4.** End with a unison prayer and/or song (small groups may return to the large group) and a period of silence, loving God and being loved *(contemplatio)*.

OTHER OPTIONAL ENDINGS:

A: In small groups: Invite each participant to offer a free prayer for the person on his or her right, in light of what the person shared previously (or to offer a prayer silently, then say an "amen" to cue the next person); continue around the group. Encourage group members to thank persons on their right and left for their prayers!

B: In small or large group: Sing a prayer, such as "Kum Ba Yah" After the *Someone's praying* stanza, invite thanksgivings in a word or phrase. After the *Someone's crying* stanza, invite intercessions. After the *Someone's singing* stanza, ask participants to stand and raise their arms in joy!*

*If you are able, or lift head slightly (to symbolize resurrection).

## RESOURCE III—Faith Finding, Faith Sharing
(For use in church, over lunch, in homes, at work)

LEADER: Briefly summarize this entire exercise and explain its purpose of connecting faith with daily life. This exercise is faith sharing "from below," so each person stands on an equal footing.

ANNOUNCE: "Choose someone with whom you will share in a few minutes—just turn to the person next to you, or all get up and mix around till everyone is linked with someone." (Invite everyone to be seated; create a quiet atmosphere.) Then announce,

STEP 1. "Reflect over the past week (or given period of time)....Notice a problem you've had to deal with in some area of your life...." Allow a few minutes of silence.

STEP 2. "Contemplate: How has God—or Christ or prayer or my faith or my community of faith—made a difference in how I responded to that problem?" (Allow a few minutes of silence. Then find a simple way to break the silence: a spoken "amen," ringing a soft bell, or a sentence prayer such as, "O God, be with us now as we share.")

STEP 3. "Meet with one other person and share the issue or concern, and reflect with your neighbor on how your faith made a difference." (Announce the length of time for sharing—six to ten minutes total, three to five minutes per person.)

STEP 4. After sharing, invite each pair now to spend one minute in *silent prayer*: "Closing your eyes, picture the face of your partner, lifting up that person's needs and gifts." (Option: "Offer a sentence prayer for each other—the discipline of *only* a sentence!") "When you are ready, give your friend some sign of Christ's peace."

STEP 5. End as seems natural with large group discussion. Ask: What did we learn about faith sharing? Conclude with a hymn or a spiritual, such as "Guide My Feet," "Amazing Grace," or "Day by Day."

## RESOURCE IV—The Worship Interview
Reinventing the Testimony

Reinvent the "witness" or "testimony," an ancient biblical tradition. One of the contemporary ways to validate people's experiences of faith is to adapt the popular interview format. Encourage laypersons to give a brief three- to five-minute witness to God at work in life. (See Resource III.)

This is how it works. A pastor, staff member, or volunteer serves as coordinator and arranges for the interviews, keeping a list of "nominations." The people participate in the "service of worship" by submitting names (with permission) of potential interviewees, who may always decline. (A shy person who has shared a powerful faith story in a women's circle or a men's group might never offer to give a official "testimony," but the interview makes it easier.) The coordinator (or someone else trained in interview methods) serves as the "host." The host talks with the interviewee to go over general themes and questions that will be asked but allows for spontaneity during the actual interview in worship (seated in chairs or standing). This process validates the "liturgy" as a celebration of God's work in people's lives and promotes faith finding and faith sharing as the norm in a life-giving church.

OPTION: *Adapt this resource for dramatic reading of scriptures.* Interviewer: "We are privileged to have the Apostle Paul with us today. Tell us, 'What was it like to lose everything?'" ("Paul" reads Philippians 3:7-10.) "Hmmm... I'm feeling inferior, like you've already arrived." ("Paul"reads 3:12-14.) "So we don't have to be perfect?" ("Paul" reads 3:15-16.)

Or use the dramatic reading of scriptures occasionally as another way of letting the Word come alive. (See LL 8.)

## RESOURCE V—Space for Grace in the Agenda

In committee meetings, give yourself and others permission to call for brief periods of silence during the agenda time. Practice "pause and pray" during the discussion.

❖ Encourage any member or the convener to call for silence to ponder and pray when discussing weighty matters, when too many words get in the way of listening—or if you feel a need to savor a moment of levity! (Let anyone break the silence with a sentence prayer, a verse of scripture, or an Amen.) After a silence, notice if there is a difference in the quality of the discussion.

❖ A call for silence is always a good way to prepare before voting on major issues.

❖ Use opportunities to put a "contemplative lens" on ordinary factual or financial reports. In my last parish over thirty names of homebound members who had received Communion were listed, yet I would read the list aloud prayerfully, prefaced by the comment, "As you hear each name, let it be a prayer for God's peace for that person."

❖ Do not leave it all to the pastor to implement: The treasurer can be encouraged to say, "Before we look at the figures, let's pause and pray for the financial stewardship of ourselves and our congregation." A mere ten seconds can reframe a factual report as a prayer!

OPTION: Try passing out picture postcards (like Van Gogh paintings or Ansel Adams photos), nature scenes, or photos of activities of your faith community—one for each person. Then before the next report ask each person to pass the picture to the person on his or her right. Pause and pray, or read a scripture verse. Or pass around a chalice, baptismal font, or clergy stole as a sign of ministry during a business meeting, or during worship (LL 31).

### RESOURCE VI—Meeting Space as Intercession

Here are *group* prayer practices for your committee or board meetings as ways of "being with" those you serve by choosing the space where you meet to be more attentive to the task as well as the persons you serve. These are hands-on ways of weaving community care (*koinonía*) into the administration (*diakonía*), worship (*leitourgía*), education (*didachê*), and outreach (*apostolê*).

❖ LAY MINISTRY COMMITTEE ("Stephen ministers" or deacons): Arrange for a regular committee meeting in a room of a local nursing home (where one of your members is a resident), a hospital, or a rehab center. If you make arrangements ahead of time, you might ask some members to sit in wheel chairs or geriatric chairs during the meeting. Begin or end the meeting with silent prayer, becoming aware of sounds, smells, sights, feelings, thoughts. Then ask members to converse about their experiences and observations.

❖ WORSHIP COMMITTEE: Occasionally try meeting in the sanctuary, the place where worship actually takes place, spending time in quiet prayer and being attentive to symbols of worship. Example: If you are discerning the frequency of Communion, try sitting in the chancel near the Communion table, on which is placed a chalice and plate. Prayerfully meditate and pray *before, during,* and *after* your discussion of the issues and agenda. Perhaps end with Communion.

❖ CHRISTIAN EDUCATION COMMITTEE: Meet in various church school rooms, the church library, etc., as a prayer for those involved in that area of learning. Example: If debating an issue concerning preschool children, use the nursery and sit in the child-size chairs (if you are able). Open with a scripture and silent meditation; invite each person to "become as a child." Invite group members to converse about their experiences and insights; sing a children's song as a prayer.

❖ WORSHIP OR CHRISTIAN EDUCATION: Meet around the baptismal font with group members telling what they know about their own baptism. Then use a brief order for "remembrance of baptism" as the group's communal prayer time.

❖ OUTREACH COMMITTEE: Arrange to hold an occasional meeting at the site of local mission projects that your church funds. Be prayerfully attentive to bulletin boards and posters, sights and sounds.Before beginning the business, take a minute of silent prayer to dedicate the group's meeting time to this particular cause.

## RESOURCE VII—Cross-Cultural Leadership "Retreat"
### (Or Advent or Lenten Study)

While theologians like Harvey Cox write about the world force of Pentecostal Christianity, you do not have to go to Kenya or Guatemala to have a cross-cultural experience. Why not encourage your church board to learn from a cross-cultural church just across town? Contact the local Nazarene or Pentecostal church to ask if some of your board members (and a spouse or friend) may attend their service. (For pastors and others not free Sunday mornings: Research some alternate worship times but also negotiate a few selected Sundays for this purpose.) Balance the perspectives: Visit an Eastern Orthodox or a Roman Catholic church, a couple of different types of African American churches, a Quaker meeting, a Korean church, a country church, an evangelical "mega-church." Visiting other faith traditions is an excellent way to begin exploring contemporary forms of worship and electronic media.[79]

*Keep an eye on what needs are being met and on the methods used for worship, education, stewardship, and leadership.* Include conversation with your hosts afterward, offering to bring refreshments or inviting them to your service. Talk about areas that could deepen yet expand your own faith tradition.

*Frame this process as an extended board retreat using Jesus' prayer: Love one another—that they all may be one.* Consider inviting a spiritual director to reflect with the board for a half day or an evening.

OPTION: Adapt this practice or a similar idea as an elective for an Advent or Lenten study group—to break the sameness of traditional study groups year after year.

## RESOURCE VIII—Spiritual Wellness for Ministry

FIVE "SPIRITUAL APTITUDES" FOR SPIRITUAL WELLNESS IN MINISTRY:

1. soul care: self-nurturance in community and solitude;
2. balance in one's schedule between sabbath and action;
3. healthy intimacy with others;
4. contemplative-active listening; and
5. creative use of "negative" emotions and experiences.

*Without the discipline of community, solitude degenerates into self-absorption and isolation; without the discipline of solitude, community degenerates into codependency and enmeshment.*

FIVE DISCIPLINES OF COMMUNITY:

1. a life-giving faith community—microchurches within the macro-church;
2. family relationships: singles, couples, and parents—and beyond one's own circle;
3. spiritual friends and mentors—with at least one intentional spiritual mentoring relationship for yourself (spiritual direction);
4. a spiritual support group; and
5. life-giving stories—faith finding and faith sharing in all contexts of ministry.

FIVE DISCIPLINES OF SOLITUDE:

1. an honest personal prayer life—including praying with scriptures, physical and spiritual exercises, journaling, centering prayer, and music (set aside time at least four days out of seven); pausing to pray several times during each day;
2. silence (at least two minutes each morning no matter how busy you are) and periodic personal retreats (at least twice a year);
3. spiritual readings and continuing learning experiences;
4. a life mission statement; and
5. ongoing discernment of one's gifts and call.

These practices create sabbath space—"to listen to Love, to love," so the Word becomes flesh in us, the body of Christ.

## RESOURCE IX—Design Your Own Lab

Design your own prayer laboratory with another person, with a board or committee, or in a retreat setting. Refer to the tapestry on the book flap.

1.  Prayerfully choose one sabbath practice you feel drawn to deepen: *prayer, discernment-vision, faith stories, silence-presence, or hospitality.*
2.  Relate that sabbath practice to one of the active ministries toward which you feel drawn: worship, administration, education, soul care, or outreach.
3.  What are the possibilities for personal growth? communal growth?

Now reverse the exercise and choose one ministry function that needs attention—a "squeaky wheel," a problem area. Ponder which sabbath practice this reflection draws you to deepen. For example, concerns for outreach might draw you to hospitality—and to befriend shamed aspects of your own soul in solitude (the tapestry's back side) and to find ways of befriending marginalized people in your community (the front side).

DESIGNING YOUR OWN LAB I—SILENT RETREAT TIME
(May be repeated for each of the five sabbath practices.) Choose one *sabbath practice* among the five listed that you feel called to deepen. How does this practice connect to a particular aspect of your ministry?
*Personal possibilities:*


*Communal possibilities:*


DESIGNING YOUR OWN LAB II—SILENT RETREAT TIME
(May be repeated for each of the five ministry functions.) Choose one ministry function among those listed that you feel called to strengthen. Which sabbath practice particularly connects with this call?
*Personal possibilities:*


*Communal possibilities:*

# Notes

1. No spiritual classic is more essential for every disciple than the little book by Brother Lawrence of the Resurrection, *The Practice of the Presence of God.*

2. This also explains why persons called to the contemplative life are engaged in service equally as active Christians, as Thomas Merton pointed out in *The Seven Storey Mountain.* We can read the story of Luke 10:38-42 in this light: Martha's service was hospitality; Mary's was listening and learning. The art is to engage in either form of service as prayer without being distracted. We can also see the two in the mystical life of Howard Thurman and the political life of Martin Luther King Jr.

3. Evelyn Underhill, *The Spiritual Life* (Harrisburg, Penn.: Morehouse Publishing, 1999), 55.

4. On willfulness and willingness, see Gerald May, *Will and Spirit* (San Francisco: Harper & Row, 1982), 316–17.

5. See Tilden Edwards, *Living in the Presence* (San Francisco: Harper & Row, 1987).

6. Howard Rice, *The Pastor as Spiritual Guide* (Nashville, Tenn.: Upper Room Books, 1998), 51.

7. Robert K. Greenleaf, *Servant Leadership: A Journey into the Nature of Legitimate Power and Greatness* (New York: Paulist Press, 1977), 239.

8. Douglas John Hall, *The End of Christendom and the Future of Christianity* (Valley Forge, Penn.: Trinity Press International, 1997), 55.

9. Harvey Cox, *Fire from Heaven: The Rise of Pentecostal Spirituality and the Reshaping of Religion in the Twenty-First Century* (New York: Addison-Wesley Publishing Co., 1995), xv.

10. Robert Wuthnow, *After Heaven: Spirituality Since the 1950s* (Berkeley: University of California Press, 1998), 17.

11. I have set these words of Mechthild of Magdeburg as an original chant in *Active Spirituality*, 175. The words are universal—used by Benedict, Ignatius, Teresa of Avila, and many others.

12. William M. Easum, "The Three Keys of Strategic Action: A Case Study," *Net Results: New Ideas in Church Vitality* 20 (March 1999): 22.

13. Howard Gardner, *Frames of Mind: The Theory of Multiple Intelligences* (New York: Basic Books, 1983), and *The Unschooled Mind: How Children Think and How Schools Should Teach* (New York: Basic Books, 1991), 10–12. See also *Creating Minds: An Anatomy of Creativity Seen through the Lives of Freud, Einstein, Picasso, Stravinsky, Eliot, Graham, and Gandhi* (New York: Basic Books, 1993).

14. Flannery O'Connor, *Mystery and Manners*, eds. Sally and Robert Fitzgerald (New York: Farrar, Straus & Giroux, 1957), 101.

15. Andre Dubus, "A Father's Story," in *Listening for God,* vol. 2, eds. Paula J. Carlson and Peter S. Hawkins (Minneapolis: Augsburg Fortress Press, 1996), 147.

16. Acts 20:7 indicates the pattern of the early church was to gather on the first day of the week "to break bread." Luther, Calvin, and Knox all advocated weekly Eucharist, which is still the unbroken pattern at St. Giles (Presbyterian) Cathedral in Edinburgh, Scotland, since Knox served as its pastor.

17. See Timothy D. Hoare, *Pulling the Siamese Dragon: Performance as a Theological Agenda for Christian Ritual Praxis* (New York: University Press of America, 1997).

18. Eugene Peterson, "Eat This Book: The Holy Community at Table with Holy Scripture," *Theology Today* 56 (April 1999): 15.

19. Brian Wren, "What Makes Worship Contemporary?" Lecture given at Lancaster Theological Seminary, September 29, 1998.

20. Suzanne Langer, *Philosophy in a New Key* (Cambridge, Mass.: Harvard University Press, 1942), 202.

21. Robert F. Crowley, *Lectionary Scenes: 57 Vignettes for Cycle A (B or C)* (Lima, Ohio: CSS Publishing Company, Inc., 1997, 1998, 1999).

22. See John S. McClure, *The Roundtable Pulpit* (Nashville, Tenn.: Abingdon Press, 1995) and Lucy Atkinson Rose, *Sharing the Word: Preaching in the Roundtable Church* (Louisville, Ky.: Westminster John Knox Press, 1997).

23. E. M. Bounds, *Power through Prayer* (London: Marshall, Morgan & Scott Ltd., n.d.), 36.

24. Paul Tillich, *The New Being* (New York: Scribner's, 1955), 138.

25. Marva J. Dawn, *Reaching Out without Dumbing Down: A Theology of Worship for the Turn-of-the-Century Culture* (Grand Rapids: Wm. B. Eerdmans Publishing Co., 1995), 265.

26. Adapted from Kent Ira Groff, *Active Spirituality: A Guide for Seekers and Ministers* (Bethesda, Md.: Alban Institute, 1993), 150–57.

27. See Acts 20:7. Both Luther and Calvin advocated weekly Communion. Tex Sample, author of *The Spectacle of Worship in a Wired World: Electronic Culture and the Gathered People of God* (Nashville, Tenn.: Abingdon Press, 1998), while advocating for electronic means of worship, also advocates weekly Communion precisely because of its participatory and multi-sensual dimensions.

28. Bounds, *Power through Prayer*, 10 (author's revision of exclusively masculine language).

29. Greenleaf, *Servant Leadership*, 239.

30. Bounds, *Power through Prayer*, 10 (author's revision of language).

31. Frederick Buechner, *Wishful Thinking: A Theological ABC* (San Francisco: Harper & Row, 1973), 95.

32. See Richard Nelson Bolles, *What Color Is Your Parachute?—A Practical Manual for Job Hunters & Career-Changers* (Berkeley, Calif.: Ten Speed Press, 1970), 355–75.

33. I follow the KJV: "If your eye is *single...*" (Greek *haplos*). The rabbis spoke of "the singling of the eye"; it means "singleness of heart" (Kierkegaard), an undivided vision focused on the one thing necessary.

34. This more ancient pattern of discernment is spelled out by Danny E. Morris and Charles M. Olsen in *Discerning God's Will Together* (Nashville, Tenn.: Upper Room Books, 1997). See chapter 4 of this book.

35. This story is adapted from Dale E. Galloway "Seven Keywords for a Successful Small-Group System" *Net Results: New Ideas in Church Vitality*, 20, no. 4 (April 1999): 1–3.

36. From *The Lafiya Guide: A Congregational Handbook for Whole-Person Health Ministry* (Elgin, Ill.: Association of Brethren Caregivers, 1993), 58.

37. Thomas P. Williamsen, *Attending to Parishioners' Spiritual Growth* (Bethesda, Md.: Alban Institute, 1997), 47.

38. David Tracy, "Traditions of Spiritual Practice and the Practice of Theology," *Theology Today* 55 (July 1998): 240–241.

39. See Workshop Rotation Web site at www.rotation.org—and users1.ee.net/sundaysoft.

40. Peterson, "Eat This Book," 13.

41. William Shakespeare, *Hamlet*, in *Shakespeare: The Complete Works*, vol. 2, ed. G.B. Harrison (New York: Harcourt, Brace, and World, Inc., 1948), 905.

42. Wade Clark Roof, quoted in Holly J. Lebowitz, "Lost and Found," from *Salon* (an online journal, www.salon.com) (9 October 1999).

43. John Westerhoff and Gwen Kennedy Neville, *Learning Through Liturgy* (New York: Seabury Press, 1978), 91–92. See also William H. Willimon, *Worship as Pastoral Care* (Nashville, Tenn.: Abingdon Press, 1979), 123–24, n. 1.

44. William H. Willimon, *Worship as Pastoral Care* (Nashville, Tenn.: Abingdon Press, 1979), 122–23.

45. Tracy, "Traditions of Spiritual Practice," 240–41. See Simone Weil, *Waiting for God* (New York: Harper Colophon Books, 1973), 105–116.

46. Albert Schweitzer, *The Quest of the Historical Jesus* (Baltimore: Johns Hopkins University Press, 1998), 403.

47. Grenaé D. Dudley and Carlyle Fielding Stewart III, *Sankofa: Celebrations for the African American Church* (Cleveland, Ohio: United Church Press, 1997), 9.

48. Marianne Sawicki, *Seeing the Lord: Resurrection and Early Christian Practices* (Minneapolis: Fortress Press, 1994), 72.

49. Kenda Creasy Dean and Ron Foster, *The Godbearing Life: The Art of Soul Tending for Youth Ministry* (Nashville, Tenn.: Upper Room Books, 1998).

50. Mark Yaconelli, "Youth Ministry: A Contemplative Approach," *The Christian Century* 116 (21–28 April 1999): 452.

51. Ibid.

52. Bengt R. Hoffman, *Luther and the Mystics* (Minneapolis: Augsburg Publishing House, 1976), 187.

53. See Richard C. Meyer, *One Anothering: Biblical Building Blocks for Small Groups* (San Diego: LuraMedia, 1990).

54. Henri J. M. Nouwen and Walter J. Gaffney, *Aging: The Fulfillment of Life* (Garden City: Doubleday/Image Books, 1974), 102 (author's adaptation).

55. Henri J. M. Nouwen, *The Living Reminder* (New York: Seabury Press, 1977), 45.

56. Joyce Rupp, *Praying Our Goodbyes* (Notre Dame, Ind.: Ave Maria Press, 1988), 83–95.

57. Sawicki, *Seeing the Lord,* 72.

58. See Larry Dossey, *Recovering the Soul: A Scientific and Spiritual Search* (New York: Bantam Books, 1989) and *Prayer Is Good Medicine* (San Francisco: HarperSanFrancisco, 1996).

59. Walter Wink, *Engaging the Powers: Discernment and Resistance in a World of Domination* (Minneapolis: Fortress Press, 1992), 299.

60. Willimon, *Worship as Pastoral Care*, 216.

61. *The Songs and Prayers of Taizé: Basic Edition* (Chicago: GIA Publishing Co., 1991). To order, write GIA Publishing Co., 7404 S. Mason Avenue, Chicago, Illinois 60638.

62. See Parker Palmer, "The Clearness Committee: A Way of Discernment," *Weavings* 3 (July/August1988): 37–40.

63. Charles M. Olsen in *Transforming Church Boards into Communities of Spiritual Leaders* (Bethesda, Md.: Alban Institute, 1995), 66-67.

64. Denise Levertov, *Sands of the Well* (New York: New Directions Publishing Corp., 1994), 18.

65. Clarissa Pinkola Estés, *Women Who Run with the Wolves: Myths and Stories of the Wild Woman Archetype* (New York: Ballantine Books, 1992), 464.

66. Canon Lauren Artress, interviewed by Nora Gallagher in *Things Seen and Unseen: A Year Lived in Faith* (New York: Alfred A. Knopf, 1998), 161.

67. Anne Lamott, *Traveling Mercies: Some Thoughts on Faith* (New York: Pantheon Books, 1999), 54–55.

68. Russell Chandler, *Feeding the Flock: Restaurants and Churches You'd Stand in Line For* (Bethesda, Md.: Alban Institute, 1998).

69. Alan C. Klaas, *In Search of the Unchurched: Why People Don't Join Your Congregation* (Bethesda, Md.: Alban Institute, 1996), 24, 47.

70. Maria Harris, *Proclaim Jubilee!: A Spirituality for the Twenty-First Century* (Louisville, Ky.: Westminster John Knox Press, 1996), 110.

71. "Three crucial issues" are based on the above-mentioned lecture at Morning Star Regional Seminary, Barrackpore, India, January 21, 1999; portions adapted in Kent Ira Groff, "Listening: Unity in Prayer and Action," *Sampriti: News Bulletin for Catholic Commission for Ecumenism* II (India, April 1999): 3–4.

72. W. E. B. Du Bois, *The Souls of Black Folk* (New York: Signet Classic, Penguin Putnam, 1995), 274.

73. Douglas V. Steere, *Work and Contemplation* (New York: Harper & Brothers, 1957), 56 (emphasis in original).

74. Garnett E. Foster, "A Model for New Member Recruitment," *Congregations: The Alban Journal* 24 (March/April 1998): 8. See also Howard Edington, *Downtown Church: The Heart of the City* (Nashville, Tenn.: Abingdon Press, 1996), 127.

75. Walter Brueggemann, "The Liturgy of Abundance, the Myth of Scarcity," *The Christian Century* 116 (24–31 March 1999): 344.

76. Parker Palmer, *The Active Life: A Spirituality of Work, Creativity, and Caring* (San Francisco: Harper & Row, 1990), 88.

77. C. S. Lewis quoted in Willimon, *Worship as Pastoral Care*, 17.

78. John. T. McNeill, ed., *The Library of Christian Classics*, Vol. XXI, *Calvin: Institutes of the Christian Religion*, trans. Ford Lewis Battles (Philadelphia: The Westminster Press, 1960), 892.

79. See Sample, *The Spectacle of Worship*.

# Bibliography

Ackerman, John. *Spiritual Awakening: A Guide to Spiritual Life in Congregations.* Bethesda, Md.: Alban Institute, 1994.

Allen, Diogenes. *Christian Belief in a Postmodern World: The Full Wealth of Conviction.* Louisville, Ky.: Westminster/John Knox Press, 1997.

Barna, George. *Turn-Around Churches: How to Overcome Barriers to Growth and Bring New Life to an Established Church.* Ventura, Calif.: Regal Books, 1997.

Bass, Dorothy C., ed. *Practicing Our Faith: A Way of Life for Searching People.* San Francisco: Jossey-Bass Publishers, 1997.

Baxter, Richard. *The Reformed Pastor.* Edited by James M. Houston. Portland, Ore.: Multnomah Press, 1982.

Beaudoin, Tom. *Virtual Faith: The Irreverent Spiritual Quest of Generation X.* San Francisco: Jossey-Bass Publishers, 1998.

Bellah, Robert N., et al. *Habits of the Heart: Individualism and Commitment in American Life.* Berkeley: University of California Press, 1985.

Biersdorf, John. *How Prayer Shapes Ministry.* Bethesda, Md.: Alban Institute, 1992.

Bolles, Richard Nelson. *What Color Is Your Parachute?—A Practical Manual for Job Hunters & Career-Changers.* Berkeley, Calif.: Ten Speed Press, 1970.

Borg, Marcus J. *Meeting Jesus Again for the First Time: The Historical Jesus and the Heart of Contemporary Faith.* San Francisco: HarperSanFrancisco, 1995.

Borg, Marcus J. and N. T. Wright. *The Meaning of Jesus: Two Visions.* San Francisco: HarperSanFrancisco, 1999.

Boschman, LaMar, C. Peter Wagner, and Judson Cornwall. *Future Worship: How a Changing World Can Enter God's Presence in the New Millennium.* Ventura, Calif.: Gospel Light Publications, 1999.

Bounds, E. M. *Power through Prayer.* London: Marshall, Morgan, & Scott Ltd., n.d.

Brother Lawrence. *The Practice of the Presence of God.* Translated by John Delaney. New York: Doubleday, 1996.

Brown, Patricia D. *Spirit Gifts,* Leader's Guide and Participant's Workbook. Nashville, Tenn.: Abingdon Press, 1996.

———. *Learning to Lead from Your Spiritual Center.* Nashville, Tenn.: Abingdon Press, 1996.

Brueggemann, Walter. "The Liturgy of Abundance, the Myth of Scarcity." *The Christian Century* 116 (24–31 March, 1999):342–347.

Buechner, Frederick. *Wishful Thinking: A Theological ABC.* San Francisco: Harper & Row, 1973.

Chandler, Russell. *Feeding the Flock: Restaurants and Churches You'd Stand in Line For.* Bethesda, Md.: Alban Institute, 1998.

Cladis, George. *Leading the Team-Based Church: How Pastors and Church Staffs Can Grow Together into a Powerful Faith.* San Francisco: Jossey-Bass Publishers, 1999.

Cobble, James F. Jr. and Charles M. Elliott, eds. *The Hidden Spirit: Discovering the Spirituality of Institutions.* Mathews, N.C.: Christian Ministry Resources, 1999. Available directly from Christian Ministry Resources, P.O. Box 1098, Mathews, NC 28106. Or call (704) 821-3845.

Costen, Melva Wilson. *African American Christian Worship.* Nashville, Tenn.: Abingdon Press, 1993.

Cox, Harvey. *Fire from Heaven: The Rise of Pentecostal Spirituality and the Reshaping of Religion in the Twenty-First Century.* New York: Addison-Wesley Publishing Co., 1995.

Crowley, Robert F. *Lectionary Scenes: 57 Vignettes for Cycle A (B or C).* Lima, Ohio: CSS Publishing Company, Inc., 1997, 1998, 1999.

Dawn, Marva J. *Reaching Out without Dumbing Down: A Theology of Worship for the Turn-of-the-Century Church.* Grand Rapids: William B. Eerdman's Publishing Co., 1995.

Dean, Kenda Creasy, and Ron Foster. *The Godbearing Life: The Art of Soul Tending for Youth Ministry.* Nashville, Tenn.: Upper Room Books, 1998.

Dossey, Larry. *Prayer Is Good Medicine.* San Francisco: HarperSanFrancisco, 1996.

———. *Recovering the Soul: A Scientific and Spiritual Search.* New York: Bantam Books, 1989.

Du Bois, W. E. B. *The Souls of Black Folk.* New York: Signet Classic, Penguin Putnam, 1995.

Dubus, Andre. "A Father's Story." In *Listening for God,* vol. 2. Edited by Paula J. Carlson and Peter S. Hawkins. Minneapolis: Augsburg Fortress Press, 1996.

Dudley, Grenaé D., and Carlyle Fielding Stewart III. *Sankofa: Celebrations for the African American Church.* Cleveland, Ohio: United Church Press, 1997.

Dykstra, Craig. *Growing in the Life of Faith: Education and Christian Practices.* Louisville, Ky.: Geneva Press, 1999.

Easum, William M. "The Three Keys of Strategic Action: A Case Study." *Net Results: New Ideas in Church Vitality* 20 (March 1999): 20–22.

Easum, William M. and Thomas G. Bandy. *Growing Spiritual Redwoods.* Nashville, Tenn.: Abingdon Press, 1997.

Edington, Howard. *Downtown Church: The Heart of the City.* Nashville, Tenn.: Abingdon Press, 1996.

Edwards, Tilden. *Living in the Presence.* San Francisco: Harper & Row, 1987.

Foster, Garnett E. "A Model for New Member Recruitment." *Congregations: The Alban Journal* 24 (March/April 1998): 8.

Foster, Richard J. *Freedom of Simplicity: Finding Harmony in a Complex World.* San Francisco: HarperSanFrancisco, 1989.

Friend, Howard G. Jr. *Recovering the Sacred Center: Church Renewal from the Inside Out.* Valley Forge, Va.: Judson Press, 1998.

Gallagher, Nora. *Things Seen and Unseen: A Year Lived in Faith.* New York: Alfred A. Knopf, 1998.

Gardner, Howard. *Frames of Mind: The Theory of Multiple Intelligences.* New York: Basic Books, 1983.

————. *The Unschooled Mind: How Children Think and How Schools Should Teach.* New York: Basic Books, 1991.

————. *Creating Minds: An Anatomy of Creativity Seen through the Lives of Freud, Einstein, Picasso, Stravinsky, Eliot, Graham, and Gandhi.* New York: Basic Books, 1993.

Greenleaf, Robert K. *Servant Leadership: A Journey into the Nature of Legitimate Power and Greatness.* New York: Paulist Press, 1977.

Groff, Kent Ira. *Active Spirituality: A Guide for Seekers and Ministers.* Bethesda, Md.: Alban Institute, 1993.

————. *Journeymen: A Spiritual Guide for Men (and for Women Who Want to Understand Them).* Nashville, Tenn.: Upper Room Books, 1999.

————. *Spirituality Matters for Committee Meetings.* Decatur, Ga.: CTS Press, 1996.

————. *Spiritual Practices for Beginners and Leaders.* Decatur, Ga.: CTS Press, 1996.

Hall, Douglas John. *The End of Christendom and the Future of Christianity.* Valley Forge, Pa.: Trinity Press International, 1997.

Harris, Maria. *Proclaim Jubilee!: A Spirituality for the Twenty-First Century.* Louisville, Ky.: Westminster John Knox Press, 1996.

Hoare, Timothy D. *Pulling the Siamese Dragon: Performance as a Theological Agenda for Christian Ritual Praxis.* New York: University Press of America, 1997.

Hoffman, Bengt R. *Luther and the Mystics.* Minneapolis: Augsburg Publishing House, 1976.

Holmes, Urban T. III. *Spirituality for Ministry.* San Francisco: Harper & Row, 1982.

Hunter, George G. III. *How to Reach Secular People.* Nashville, Tenn.: Abingdon Press, 1992.

Johnson, Ben Campbell. *Speaking of God: Evangelism as Initial Spiritual Guidance.* Louisville, Ky.: Westminster John Knox Press, 1991.

Johnson, Luke Timothy. *Scripture and Discernment: Decision Making in the Church.* Nashville, Tenn.: Abingdon Press, 1996.

Keifert, Patrick R. *Welcoming the Stranger: A Public Theology of Worship and Evangelism.* Minneapolis: Augsburg Fortress Press, 1992.

Klaas, Alan C. *In Search of the Unchurched: Why People Don't Join Your Congregation*. Bethesda, Md.: Alban Institute, 1996.

*The Lafiya Guide: A Congregational Handbook for Whole-Person Health Ministry*. Elgin, Ill.: Association of Brethren Caregivers, 1993.

Lamott, Anne. *Traveling Mercies: Some Thoughts on Faith*. New York: Pantheon Books, 1999.

Langer, Suzanne. *Philosophy in a New Key*. Cambridge, Mass.: Harvard University Press, 1942.

Larson, Bruce, and Ralph Osborne. *The Emerging Church*. Waco, Tex.: Word Books, 1970.

Levertov, Denise. *Sands of the Well*. New York: New Directions Publishing Corp., 1994.

May, Gerald. *Will and Spirit*. San Francisco: Harper & Row, 1982.

McClure, John S. *The Roundtable Pulpit*. Nashville, Tenn.: Abingdon Press, 1995.

Mead, Loren. *The Once and Future Church*. Bethesda, Md.: Alban Institute, 1992.

———. *Five Challenges for the Once and Future Church*. Bethesda, Md., Alban Institute, 1996.

Meyer, Richard C. *One Anothering: Biblical Building Blocks for Small Groups*. San Diego: Lura-Media, 1990.

Miller, Kim and the Ginghamsburg Church Worship Design Team. *Handbook for Multi-Sensory Worship*. Nashville, Tenn.: Abingdon Press, 1999.

Morgenthaler, Sally. *Worship Evangelism: Inviting Unbelievers into the Presence of God*. Grand Rapids: Zondervan Publishing Co., 1999.

Morley, Barry. *Beyond Consensus: Salvaging Sense of the Meeting*. Wallingford, Penn.: Pendle Hill, 1993.

Morris, Danny E., and Charles M. Olsen. *Discerning God's Will Together: A Spiritual Practice for the Church*. Nashville, Tenn.: Upper Room Books and Bethesda, Md.: Alban Institute, 1997.

Nouwen, Henri J. M. *Creative Ministry*. New York: Doubleday, 1971.

———. *The Living Reminder*. New York: The Seabury Press, 1977.

Nouwen, Henri J. M., and Walter J. Gaffney. *Aging: The Fulfillment of Life*. Garden City: Doubleday/Image Books, 1974.

O'Connor, Flannery. *Mystery and Manners*. Edited by Sally and Robert Fitzgerald. New York: Farrar, Straus & Giroux, 1957.

Olsen, Charles M. *Transforming Church Boards into Communities of Spiritual Leaders*. Bethesda, Md.: Alban Institute, 1995.

Palmer, Parker J. "The Clearness Committee: A Way of Discernment." *Weavings* 3 (July/August 1988): 37–40.

Peterson, Eugene. *The Contemplative Pastor*. Grand Rapids: William B. Eerdman's Publishing Co., 1993.

———. "Eat This Book: The Holy Community at Table with Holy Scripture." *Theology Today* 56 (April 1999): 5–17.

Pritchard, John. *The Intercession Handbook: Creative Ideas for Public and Private Prayer.* London, SPCK, 1998.

Rediger, G. Lloyd. *Clergy Killers: Guidance for Pastors and Congregations under Attack.* Inver Grove Heights, Minn.: Logos Productions, 1996.

Reeves, Donald. *Down to Earth.* New York: Mowbray, A Cassell Imprint, 1966.

Rice, Howard. *The Pastor as Spiritual Guide.* Nashville, Tenn.: Upper Room Books, 1998.

Robinson, Gnana. *Deeper Spirituality.* Chennai, India: The Literature Society, 1999.

Roof, Wade Clark. Quoted in Holly J. Lebowitz, "Lost and Found" in *Salon* (an online journal, www.salon.com) (9 October, 1999).

Rose, Lucy Atkinson. *Sharing the Word: Preaching in the Roundtable Church.* Louisville, Ky.: Westminster John Knox Press, 1997.

Rupp, Joyce. *Praying Our Goodbyes.* Notre Dame, Ind.: Ave Maria Press, 1988.

Sample, Tex. *Hard Living People and Mainstream Christians.* Nashville, Tenn.: Abingdon Press, 1993.

————. *Ministry in an Oral Culture: Living with Will Rogers, Uncle Remus, and Minnie Pearl.* Louisville, Ky.: Westminster/John Knox Press, 1994.

————. *The Spectacle of Worship in a Wired World: Electronic Culture and the Gathered People of God.* Nashville, Tenn.: Abingdon Press, 1998.

Sawicki, Marianne. *Seeing the Lord: Resurrection and Early Christian Practices.* Minneapolis: Fortress Press, 1994.

Schweitzer, Albert. *The Quest of the Historical Jesus.* Baltimore: Johns Hopkins University Press, 1998.

Sider, Ronald J. *Cup of Water, Bread of Life: Inspiring Stories about Overcoming Lopsided Christianity.* Grand Rapids: Zondervan Publishing House, 1994.

Sine, Tom. *Mustard Seed versus McWorld: Reinventing Life and Faith for the Future.* Grand Rapids: Baker Book House, 1999.

Smith, James Bryan, Richard Foster and Linda Graybeal. *A Spiritual Formarmation Workbook: Small Group Resources for Nurturing Christian Growth.* New York: HarperCollins, 1999.

*Songs and Prayers of Taizé: Basic Edition.* Chicago: GIA Publishing Co., 1991.

*Spiritual Manifestos: Visions for Renewed Religious Life in America from Young Spiritual Leaders of Many Faiths.* Edited by Niles Goldstein. Woodstock, Vt.: Skylight Paths Publishing, 1999.

Steere, Douglas V. *Work and Contemplation.* New York: Harper & Brothers, 1957.

Tillich, Paul. *The New Being.* New York: Scribner's, 1955.

Tracy, David. "Traditions of Spiritual Practice and the Practice of Theology." *Theology Today* 55 (July 1998): 240–241.

Underhill, Evelyn. *The Spiritual Life.* Harrisburg, Pa.: Morehouse Publishing, 1999.

Warren, Rick. *The Purpose-Driven Church.* Grand Rapids: Zondervan Publishing House, 1995.

Webber, Robert E. *Ancient-Future Faith: Rethinking Evangelicalism for a Postmodern World.* Grand Rapids: Baker Book House, 1999.

————. *Liturgical Evangelism: Worship as Outreach and Nurture.* Harrisburg, Pa.: Morehouse Publishing, 1986.

————. *Planning Blended Worship: The Creative Mixture of Old and New.* Nashville, Tenn.: Abingdon Press, 1998.

Weil, Simone. *Waiting for God.* New York: Harper Colophon Books, 1973.

Westerhoff, John, and Gwen Kennedy Neville. *Learning through Liturgy.* New York: Seabury Press, 1978.

Willamsen, Thomas P. *Attending to Parishioners' Spiritual Growth.* Bethesda, Md.: Alban Institute, 1997.

Willimon, William H. *Worship as Pastoral Care.* Nashville, Tenn.: Abingdon Press, 1979.

Wren, Brian. "What Makes Worship Contemporary?" Lecture given at Lancaster Theological Seminary, September 29, 1998.

Wren, Brian. *Praying Twice: The Music of Congregational Song.* Louisville, Ky.: Westminster John Knox Press, 2000.

Wuellner, Flora Slosson. *Feed My Shepherds: Spiritual Healing and Renewal for Those in Christian Leadership.* Nashville, Tenn.: Upper Room Books, 1998.

Wuthnow, Robert. *After Heaven: Spirituality Since the 1950s.* Berkeley: University of California Press, 1998.

Yaconelli, Mark. "Youth Ministry: A Contemplative Approach." *The Christian Century* 116 (21–28 April, 1999):450–452.

Yancey, Philip. *The Jesus I Never Knew.* Grand Rapids: Zondervan Publishing House, 1995.

Young, Pamela Dickey. *Christ in a Post-Christian World: How Can We Believe in Jesus Christ When Those around Us Believe Differently—or Not at All? A Feminist Answer.* Minneapolis: Augsburg Fortress Press, 1995.

————. *Re-creating the Church: Communities of Eros.* Harrisburg, Pa.: Trinity Press International, 2000.

# Index

# Credits

## About the author

KENT IRA GROFF, an ordained Presbyterian minister, is founder and director of Oasis Ministries for Spiritual Development. Oasis Ministries is an interdenominational, nonprofit corporation that seeks to renew the spiritual life of individuals, congregations, and institutions through retreats, spiritual direction, and training programs. He is also adjunct professor at Lancaster Theological Seminary in Pennsylvania.

The author has served as a parish pastor and chaplain. He is an associate of Holy Cross Monastery, West Park, New York. He holds degrees from Pennsylvania State University (BA), Princeton Theological Seminary (M.Div.), and Chicago Theological Seminary (Doctor of Religion). Dr. Groff is also a graduate of Shalem Institute for Spiritual Formation in Bethesda, Maryland; and he completed his chaplain residency at University Hospital, Hershey Medical Center of Pennsylvania State University.

Kent is the author of *Journeymen: A Spiritual Guide for Men (and for Women Who Want to Understand Them), Active Spirituality: A Guide for Seekers and Ministers,* along with other books and numerous articles in religious periodicals. Kent is an avid poet and composer, and is married to Fredrika Simpson Groff. They have three adult children: James, Kendra, and Elizabeth.

You may schedule retreats or contact the author at Oasis Ministries, 419 Deerfield Road, Camp Hill, PA 17011; Web site: www.oasismin.org.